11

COUNTERPOINT

COUNTER POINT: DANIEL LIBES KIND

IN CONVERSATION WITH
PAUL GOLDBERGER

THE MONACELLI PRESS

CONTENTS

PUBLISHED IN THE UNITED STATES BY THE MONACELLI PRESS,
A DIVISION OF RANDOM HOUSE, INC., NEW YORK

THE MONACELLI PRESS AND THE COLOPHON ARE
TRADEMARKS OF RANDOM HOUSE, INC.

LIBRARY OF CONGRESS CATALOGING-IN-PUBLICATION DATA
LIBESKIND, DANIEL, DATE.
COUNTERPOINT : DANIEL LIBESKIND IN CONVERSATION WITH PAUL GOLDBERGER. — 1ST ED.
P.   CM.
ISBN 978-1-58093-206-6
1. LIBESKIND, DANIEL, DATE—INTERVIEWS. 2. ARCHITECTS—UNITED STATES—INTERVIEWS.
3. LIBESKIND, DANIEL, DATE—THEMES, MOTIVES. I. GOLDBERGER, PAUL. II. TITLE.
NA737.L46A35 2008
720.92—DC22   2008024340

10 9 8 7 6 5 4 3 2 1
FIRST EDITION

PRINTED IN CHINA

WITH THANKS TO LYNN KROGH FOR HER EFFORTS IN ASSEMBLING THIS BOOK

DESIGNED BY PENTAGRAM

WWW.MONACELLIPRESS.COM

To the passionate architects who worked on these projects, and to the one and only Nina.

The struggle of man against power is the struggle of memory against forgetting.
    —Milan Kundera

Daniel, your practice is now a huge operation with a main office in New York, and other offices in Zurich and Milan. It's a big enterprise. A dozen years ago or so, there was only a handful of employees and a small amount of work, and the nature of that work was more academic and theoretical. How did the transition evolve from small and academic to large and, in many ways, more commercial?

I like to think it's a natural evolution of a practice. I started with a single building: the Jewish Museum Berlin. I never built a building before. But even when I was doing what seemed to others to be abstract drawings, I never thought of them as theoretical but as somehow part of an investigation of architecture.

The curve has gone very much more dramatically upward.

I know that many architects would think that the object of their career is to build a museum. I have been fortunate to build a great number. But architecture has to engage in the whole spectrum of needs, such as housing, shopping, education, and office buildings. I certainly love the expanded opportunities. In fact, I try to blur the lines between these different typologies in order to see what is common between them as the art of architecture. I used to do one project at a time, but now I'm equally and intensely involved with many projects. I never enjoyed doing just a sketch of a concept and handing it over to others.

You had anticipated my next question, which is one of management and administration. How is it possible for one man to be completely involved in all of the work in an office as large and as diverse as this now is?

Well, first of all, I have Nina, who is a master at managing the complex operations of the studio. And of course, I am supported by extraordinarily bright and talented young architects from all over the world. In architecture, different projects are not done at the same time. If you have thirty projects, some are at the conceptual stage, some in development, some in working drawings, some in construction. So the demands are not beyond what I can do.

It's sometimes hard to explain that even in this scope of practice, I'm still designing every window, checking every form, and coordinating every detail—making sure that each building is a hand-crafted work. And that's what I love to do! If I wasn't doing that, if I didn't allow myself to do that, I wouldn't enjoy it. The diversity of different projects, in fact, finds unexpected connections and leads to new discoveries. The complexity of practice often subverts the prejudice of theory. So the mix has enriched my world view and hasn't reduced it.

What you're saying, I think, is that everyone, or most of your clients, seeks from you something that they don't have, something that will make them complete and whole.

That's true—they don't pick me out of a phone book! Seriously, they come deliberately because they want something unexpected. And perhaps something imbued with another quality. Very often, the divide between commercial and cultural projects is not as great as we think, because cultural projects aim at financial success just as much as commercial projects aim at cultural sophistication.

Is it possible that as your practice grows larger and your buildings become more common there's a risk of them becoming less unexpected and less surprising?

Well, that's a provocative thought. The truth is that there is always a danger when you become well practiced at something. To remain fresh, to make each project really relate to its site, not to become jaded or formulaic, is a challenge. But it's a good challenge, just as it is for writers and composers and poets. While they create large bodies of work, you can still recognize each artist by the individual signature. Their individuality and originality is still apparent.

Right, right. With the same language.

With the same language, yes, but with a language that is expanding its potential to communicate. That's not a drawback, it's an amplifier, because if you work at a certain new scale, you expose yourself to the unknown. Were you to work always at a small scale or a large scale, become an expert on museums or shopping centers, you would have a skewed view of architectural reality.

I know Frank Gehry has complained sometimes that clients come to him wanting Bilbao, but he feels he's beyond that and he wants to keep pushing himself. He wants to keep pushing his own creativity. Have you ever had a client say to you, say, I just saw Denver, I want one just like that, but you wanted to do something different?

That's not true for me. Perhaps it's just the opposite. No one has ever asked me to replicate any of my buildings. Perhaps the reason for that is that each of these buildings is extremely specific and doesn't suggest that it could be easily transported to another setting.

In an age of globalization, when architecture gets homogenized and flattened by the same computer-generated software, I resist this direction. I never believed in Mies van der Rohe's dictum, which was to design one building and endlessly refine it. That's a great formula for financial security, but for me it's unadventurous.

Once one studies your buildings carefully and gets closer to them, one discovers that there is a language that you've created, and within that language, in fact, there are many variations possible.

That's true. I think that the opportunity to engage in that language is a huge one. You know, if Bach didn't get so many commissions from churches and from royalty, from princes, dukes, aristocrats, he might have been a much poorer composer. It's the social engagement, it's meeting people, it's meeting clients, it's being in diverse environments that enriches your own sense of your limitations, expands your possibilities, enhances your language, makes it possible for you to develop your own work.

When you talk of Bach's commissions, you bring another interesting question to mind: the whole issue of response to clients. You are thought of as an architect with a very clear and definite point of view. Nobody comes to you because they want blandness or because they expect, as a client, that they will determine everything. What are your relationships to clients? How much do you want them to bring to you and how much do they expect from you?

Clients who come to me certainly have an ambition beyond the average—they are willing to take a risk. They are not coming to me for another consumer item!

My relationship with clients is not adversarial. Quite the opposite. I enjoy working with clients. I like to ask the client, What do you want? What kind of world do you want to create? And I enjoy the interaction. I actually think it enriches the possibilities to draw the client into their own visions, their own dreams. We share an aspiration and mutual desire to create something lasting, something successful, something beautiful.

Many architects feel that out of that dialogue, in fact, comes better work.

The dialogue is not a fairy tale. Sometimes it's fraught with tension. The pressure a client brings to bear on a project makes you distill your ideas. It's like an olive press, which comes up against the resistance of the pit and thus distills the oil. It's paradoxical that the pressure is positive. Perhaps that's the difference between theory and practice!

And out of conversation come ideas that you might not have had.

Definitely. You need the conversation. Clients form the frame within which you have to operate. I worked for many years on the Jewish Museum in Berlin, where I had no clear client. It was very difficult to design with no clear program and no informed response.

Your client had almost no program.

That's not quite true. The problem was that there were too many different options for what the museum should be. The program kept on changing. With every change of government, with every change of minister, with the earth-shattering change of unification, came new ideas. And yet, for me what was important was to maintain the integrity of the design in a turbulent time. I believed that the architecture for the Jewish Museum Berlin should communicate the depth of German-Jewish history—whatever the stated program. I strove to communicate that story, across the devastation of the Holocaust and beyond, through a building. Whatever the program, the Void, the Holocaust Tower, the Garden of Exile, the turns of history would always be there.

It's true, is it not, that there's a certain self-selecting process among clients. The clients who are likely to be the most insensitive to these issues are not likely to choose you.

That's not always been the case. The competition for the Jewish Museum was anonymous with more than 180 entrants. So being selected was in the nature of the unpredictable. Since that was my first building, this unpredictable path has been a kind of constant in my life. What's important is how you begin, and in my case, I didn't begin through apprenticeship, a job, or a network. I began with competitions.

The intellectual stimulation of the program and the situation—is that a factor?

I always rethink the program and the situation. A building without an idea is just a machine, a refrigerator on the horizon. I would not be interested in designing that. An idea can revolutionize a discourse about a building.

Architecture is something other than technology. I didn't come to architecture because I was interested in the technique of curtain walls or the depth of floor plates. For me, a building is a medium to tell a story. It's not only about itself. Buildings that are only about themselves are a bit like Narcissus falling in love with his own image. In that sense to retain a naiveté you have to try to see each project as completely fresh. That's hard to

do. The more you know—for example, zoning, costs, and fire codes—the more danger there is that your brain gets calcified!

I try to avoid the "all-knowingness" of experts in order to preserve a realm of freedom. Through hand drawing, whether it's a watercolor, a sketch, a quick pencil drawing, or a model of torn paper, the architectural idea has to have the capacity to evoke something of the work. What is this? How is it ever going to be constructed? I never start with the computer. I don't even know how to work on a computer. I draw, and then I share my ideas with the team. I begin in a very imaginative world and try not to be swayed by hackneyed formulas. But I agree, it's more and more of a challenge. The more you know, the more you have to fight against that knowledge in order to bring something original and something interesting into the world of architecture.

That is a problem, I think, one has in almost any field as one grows older and more successful. There is the tendency to sort of believe in your own eminence. It's a very important thing to work against that.

I'm a self-critical person. Very often, I'm working on a project and things are going smoothly when I realize that this "smoothness" is a trap. Architecture that just glides into reality is not for me. I don't like the slick, effortless production of a building that only needs a stylized form here and there to make it look trendy. So again, one has to be self-critical rather than pander to critics.

I think a lot of it emerges from one's general sensibility, too. My sense of you is that not only do you approach every project as new, as you just said, but you sort of wake up and approach each day as new.

It's true.

And that's your nature.

Lewis Carroll wrote in *Alice in Wonderland* that you have to do six impossible things before breakfast. It's a Talmudic thought, to be sure. The world is never the same; every second is a new world. Architecture is very slow to change in comparison with a thought, a brush stroke, a note. I try to quicken it. Otherwise it's not worth it.

Then it's a job.

Then it's a job. And I've always rebelled against just having a job. The people who work with me feel the same way. It's an adventure. You don't really know exactly where it's going to lead. It's always a kind of risk as well, because not traveling the safe route can be a rocky ride. But it's worth it.

Because how could it be otherwise?

Exactly. Otherwise it's dead—the project is dead on arrival. But that's no fun! The routine of architecture with its prosaic everydayness can be spiritually draining. If the work is to retain a spirit, it has to enter a creative process that is not linear. Although there is a defined goal, there are many unexpected paths to traverse.

I think it's essential to the creative process to believe in things as always new and as challenges and adventures. If not, what is the point of all of this?

You know, I've always thought that the clichés of any success are wrong. There are many gurus who tell you to have a goal in your life. I prefer to follow a mysterious path without being derailed. You might not know exactly where this path is going to lead you, but if you stick to it, it can be a fantastic adventure.

And it's a journey.

Yes. It's a journey where you can encounter the eternal in time.

I'd like to talk a little bit more about that very notion of your journey. Your work early in your career, as we have said, was heavily theoretical. You have become much more interested in communicating to a broader audience. I know that Nina has been an important transition in helping you come to that realization.

In terms of my career as an architect, I created drawings that, despite the fact that they appear very self-referential and obscure, were actual attempts to link architecture to a situation without a client. These were not fantasy projects but architectural explorations. The series "Micromegas" and "Chamberworks," as well as my machines, have a direct bearing on what I do today. They have embedded themselves in my own experience, and I use them continuously within my present architectural work. In fact, these are the scores through which I orchestrate present commissions.

I don't believe in the split between theory and practice, just as I don't believe in the immunity of architecture from its social and economic reality.

Do you feel as if, when a building is turned over to a client and finished, you have lost a certain control over it?

No. I don't have that proprietary feeling toward my projects. They pass into the world, but they have their own life. In a strange way, architecture is really an unfinished thing, because even though the building is finished, it takes on a new life. It becomes part of a new dynamic: how people will occupy it, use it, think about it. And I think that's the beautiful part of architecture, that it is so much part of our lives, that it is not just an object but has a soul-like aspect to it—a post-existence beyond the material reality embedded in it.

At Ground Zero, you were not able to realize any actual buildings on the site, only the overall master plan. And there was certainly a powerful narrative to that, which I think has been somewhat compromised as it has evolved.

As the master planner of Ground Zero, I brought to the site a vision that has a powerful and meaningful narrative—one that brought consensus to the turmoil of politics and emotion. Shaping Ground Zero in a spiritual way, bringing something positive to that site after such a horrendous tragedy, was what kept me going. I jumped into the fray, and as difficult as it was, I believed and still believe that the public process with all its strengths and weaknesses was the right way to go. Democracy is messy. I grew up under Communism and have no tolerance for the "grand projects" that insulate themselves from the public process. They may be architecturally impressive, but ethically they are dubious.

Even though you mention compromise, I don't consider it a dirty word. On balance, I feel that I've done the right thing, that the project is moving in the right direction. One of the biggest challenges was how to keep the site public, how in the face of incredible density Ground Zero could still retain the sense of memory. The memorial is central, the slurry wall is revealed, the Wedge of Light is implemented, the Freedom Tower is 1776 feet high, and the spiral towers emblematic of the Torch of Liberty create an unprecedented neighborhood toward the Hudson.

The plan, despite its division of labor with different architects, developers, investors, politicians, and authorities, has a unity of purpose, a unity of meaning. Of course, each piece of the master plan, each building, has its own expression and that's fine. I think that's good for the site. I guess what I'm trying to say can be best expressed by a musical analogy. You don't have to be a composer and a performer at the same time. You can be a conductor of an orchestra, who stands on the stage, knows the score, moves his hands and his body, and makes sure that all of the 120 musicians are playing the right notes with the right tonality and volume and interpretation. So that's the master plan. You're not always in control of each and every note, but you have to stand there and make sure that there's a harmony between the very disparate parts. And I believe that's my role, and I think that's the struggle. It's going to be a very inspiring and meaningful environment. That's what I believe in.

This may seem like an odd transition, given the metaphor you've just used, but I was going to ask you about the role music has played in your life.

I see architecture as musical. When I look at buildings, I don't just see them as planes, two-dimensional or three-dimensional projections. I see them as a musical composition. I hear them acoustically. Architecture is a world of relationships that is very, very close to my experience as a performing musician. My own response is that architecture, the way it's produced and received, is very similar to music. Because music is very precise. Every note is exactly where it has to be. It's extremely structured. Yet its impact is totally emotional. If the music is good, if you play it well, nobody thinks of the internal details that comprise it.

People just enjoy it, which is the same thing as with architecture. Everything is constructed from very geometric, very precise, almost scientific vibrations. And then if the architecture is good, you just see a space, which speaks to you, which moves you in some new direction. In that sense, even though I stopped being a performer musically, I use the same logical and physical sort of coordination to create a drawing, to execute the drawing, and to make sure that the building will perform over a long period of time.

That's a wonderful way to look at it. What you're saying, in effect, is that you must master great technical proficiency to create an emotional response.

Yes, that's right. The technical aspects are subservient to the whole, to the feeling of space, to the atmosphere. And if a building is truly good, it creates the feeling that you belong to it and that it speaks to you personally. I'm not interested in an architecture that makes a fetish of technology and glorifies the neutral.

Would you like some day to do a concert hall?

I would love to do that in earnest. In the Wohl Centre at Bar-Ilan University, I created an intimate multipurpose hall. In the Glass Courtyard of the Jewish Museum Berlin, I built a hall that is acoustically sophisticated, although it has many other functions. And on the docklands in Dublin, I am building a performing arts center for 2,200 people. This hall is primarily for musical and popular entertainment. It's flanked by two office blocks that made it possible to finance the hall. It's an incredibly interesting mix of culture and commerce.

And you're doing the hall.

Yes, I'm designing the hall, which is a challenge given the strict economic constraints of the developer. But acoustics are important not only for a music hall but for every building. Interestingly, our sense of balance and relationship to gravity and to the ground lies in our ears and not in our eyes. When I am designing a building, I don't just think of what it will look like, I think about its sound. Sometimes, I think it is better to listen to a building than to photograph it! What is the sound of spaces? The Void that cuts across the whole of the Jewish Museum in Berlin, for example, was a response to a particular aporia in Schoenberg's *Moses and Aaron.*

Let's go back to the Jewish Museum, which you touched on a moment ago, and talk about its symbolism and also its effect. How did that commission come to be? What was your response to this unusual situation, where it was not a clearly defined client, not a clearly defined program?

Actually it wasn't a commission, it was a competition, and when I entered it, it wasn't even about a Jewish museum but about a small department within a larger city museum. I rebelled against this idea with all my mind, body, and soul. I did not believe that the Jewish dimension should be treated like just any other department of the museum. I thought of the great contribution that Jews had made to Germany's culture, economics, science, and daily life and what the abyss of the Holocaust signified for the future.

I think there are two projects in my career as an architect that were projects that I did not, in any way, have to research or go to the library for—the Jewish Museum Berlin and Ground Zero. Both were sort of viscerally part of my background, part of my experience, part of who I am. Moving to Germany on the spur of the moment to try to realize the museum was considered a piece of madness by our friends and family. But we didn't move to Germany for a job. We moved with a belief that architecture can embody and communicate the meaning of the past and hope for the future.

What a crazy idea to think that such a thing could happen in this world—but it happened! Through luck or through who knows what this building happened despite all the predictions to the contrary. It took thirteen years from the competition to the opening of the building, and it taught me that architecture is a marathon and not a sprint! That you have to believe, fight, and persist despite adverse opinions, expedient journalists, and fickle politicians.

Somehow an idea for a building has to have its own destiny. This building became

the Jewish Museum for all of Germany, and I am gratified that it attracts young visitors from all over. By its presence, it contributes to the awareness of evils both past and present and has become a beacon of hope in the new German capital.

And you staked your life on it and it worked.

Yes. It was a real risk and it took so many years to be completed.

How did you do that?

I have no idea. I look in retrospect and I wonder how we spent thirteen years trying to build one building. Sometimes life is more fantastic than our reasoning about it.

What was the most important thing you discovered about Jewish history in Berlin or in Germany?

Jewish history is a living tradition whose flame can unexpectedly illuminate. So despite the nonreversible, the unfathomable extermination of six million Jews in the Holocaust and the persistence of anti-Semitism, despite this, you can create a building that casts a new light onto the future, because history is always developing. It's not really a story with a good or bad ending because it's a drama in whose outcome we play a part.

Do you feel that you, yourself, are more optimistic as a person than you were before?

I would say yes. Ironically, the difficulties of realizing the museum and the confrontation of my own history as the son of Holocaust survivors reaffirmed the Jewish belief that life prevails over tragedies.

I've always thought that that building is also respectful of Jewish tradition in a couple of other ways. First, it seems to me as though it is about questions more than answers. There is no catechism from that building. Much is simply unknowable.

It's true. The building doesn't say, Okay, this is depressing and now let's go and see something positive. It's more a conversation and dialogue with the visitors. The conversation is as complex as the history it displays.

The other thing that I am so struck by when I visit is that it seems to work both on a metaphorical ground but also as pure architecture space. Ultimately it needs to be to work in that visceral way that a good space does.

Architectural space, as I see it, has to be part of the story it's trying to communicate. It's not just a container to be filled; it's part of the symbolism of the building. And the symbol transports you beyond the material reality and, in architecture, toward that which language itself cannot fully articulate.

And another thing that I admire about the building is how successfully you avoided what could have happened if it had gone a little bit too far the other way, which would leave people with a feeling that this is bizarre.

Funny that you should say that! For a long time, the critical opinion was that this building did go too far, but I believe that any building has to go a certain distance in order to free itself from conventions that very often merely confirm our habits, which are simply mechanisms that allow us to forget. The zigzag of the Jewish Museum is unprecedented and has imprinted itself in the body of Berlin.

Let's pick up on that idea of context for a moment.

I feel that context is not something that is necessarily immediately accessible. Most people think that they know the context, but context is not only the thing that you see around, it's also something deep under the ground or just beyond the horizon. Context is not only who currently lives on or near a site, it's also the history of that place, the memory of those who once lived there. In that sense, the context is visible, but a lot of it is not accessible just through sight. You have to find out more about it. And that's the beauty of cities. They are themselves works of art across a very long period of time.

I felt that in two of your museums that I've visited recently. One is, of course, Denver, which opened in 2006. And earlier this very month, I

was in Toronto and went to visit the ROM and was taken by the director all the way through it.

I responded in two very different ways, each related to the context. Both projects were expansions, and I was very interested in how to grapple with the historic museum buildings. Most of the museums I've designed have been part of important historical sites.

In Toronto, I inserted the Crystal into the frame provided by the historic limestone buildings. I placed the building like a jewel into the setting without touching the old fabric. So the new construction of the Crystal is independent of the historic building. In Denver, I contrasted the titanium-clad Hamilton Wing with Gio Ponti's glass-tiled museum towers. In both cases, I sought to revitalize the existing by marking a clear delineation in time.

I don't believe in fake historicism, which glues a cornice here or puts a nice glass wall there. Even when I cut through historic trusses—as in the Contemporary Jewish Museum in San Francisco—I do so to expose and feature the craftsmanship of the past and thematize a living history.

Let's talk for a moment about the V&A, which unfortunately did not get built.

I regret that the V&A didn't get built. I worked on it for many years and loved the project. But all is not lost. For me, architecture is a laboratory of ideas that once developed can

inform other projects. I don't think I could ever have built the Denver Art Museum or the Crystal without the spatial and tectonic discoveries I made with the Spiral of the V&A.

I'd like to talk about museums themselves and how you feel your museums work. In Denver, in many cases they've created walls and partitions within your spaces. The exhibit designer there is somebody who has a great deal of sympathy and respect for your work so it's been smooth. In Toronto, the collections consist more of objects and it's somewhat easier to deal with complex spaces and objects. How conscious were you, as you designed, about the issues of display within the museum?

That's an incredibly important question. First of all, let me say that I never design the spaces in museums in a vacuum. I work very closely with the curators, with the operational directors, and with the directors of the museums. It's not as if I do something and say, Okay, now fill it. I discuss it very closely. In the case of the Denver Museum, I was never asked to do a box. There was another aspiration. The museum wanted large, flexible volumes that could be adaptable to many different uses. In Toronto, the programmatic requirements were very different because the museum was to hold objects of nature and cultural collections. But the fact is that every museum erects walls and partitions. Even elegant glass boxes need walls and partitions. That's what museums do, all the time, over and over. It's not a new phenomenon.

My view has been that a museum has to work in different ways, in many different ways—conventional, more classical ways, of course, and new, more interactive ways. Indeed, I have never been asked to do a classical museum for Renaissance paintings! Probably the walls would not all be slanted. The point is to design spaces that fit the

program and needs. In the newer museums I have worked on, certainly the purpose is very inventive. The museums are very clear that they want a synergy between new contemporary collections and different opportunities for the curators.

Just recently, I was in Denver to see the installation of the Louvre show in the changing exhibition galleries. I thought it was beautifully put together—paintings and objects—and it worked wonderfully well on two different floors. Likewise, the Dinosaur Galleries in the Crystal look spectacular in the spaces designed for them. I always feel that the architect has to respond to the client's needs. And the percentage of conventional space, let's say, versus unconventional has been very clearly given to me as an architect. I did not invent it. I would have never dared to design things that the museum would say, Oh my God, how are we going to use this? So sometimes the perception of the public is not on par with the vision of the museum to expand the visitor's experience and take the museum into the twenty-first century. I guess I believe that if a museum has a mission to foster and nurture imagination and creativity, then it would be ironic if the architecture of the museum is just another has-been formula.

I know in both cases the directors were tremendously proud of having been, in effect, your colleague in the creation. What about San Francisco, which is brand-new?

It is the same with the Contemporary Jewish Museum in San Francisco. I have worked for many years with the director to respond to the different programs. This is a museum with no permanent collection, so it requires spaces that will work for both traveling exhibitions and site-specific installations. The CJM is in a very tight space within a nineteenth-century power substation behind historic facades and skylights, partly within the space of an

existing twentieth-century hotel, and in an urban setting of a cluster of high-rise towers. The design is not just an adaptive reuse of a building. It's really a trialogue of many voices.

You touched on a very important point, it seems to me, a moment ago. Beyond what they do internally, your buildings have a presence as an enlivening force. We've surely seen that in Denver.

Well, I believe that a building is a sculpture on an urban level. I consider it a dramatic figure whose presence can be transformative. The dynamism of a building can foreshadow a development far beyond its limited footprint. For example, I am designing the Museum of Contemporary Art of Milan, which takes the famous Leonardo figure inscribed in the circle and the square and then rotates and transforms it into a volume that rises obliquely within a beautiful landscape. A building can open the world. It's almost like a painting. Within a frame, the painting is very limited, just a canvas with some paint. But a painting can open up a whole world. I think that's also the case even for people who don't enter the museum. Seeing it, having it in their city, still has an effect on the cultural sensibility. I guess I think of my buildings as windows, as magnifying glasses or telescopes of the city.

You know, we've talked a lot about museums in particular and about the way in which you've responded to different museums' programs and so forth. What we didn't talk that much about was the creative process itself. In other words, how do you translate a program and a client's needs and aspirations into your own very personal design language? How does that transition, that act, occur?

I'm not sure I'm able to make it clear. But it's a combination, first of all, of the objective facts of a project. You have to absorb the site. You have to absorb all the data, the economics of a project. You have to understand the technical aspects. But then there is a whole other

sort of operation, which is how all of that gets lifted, so to speak, by wings of the imagination or something else like that.

Without inspiration (and that's a discredited word today!), architecture would be just busy work. I guess what I'm trying to say is that inspiration comes forth from an unpredictable source buried in an unknown place. It is the encounter of this inspiration with the real facts of the project that forges the result. That's the difference between building and architecture.

I believe that at the end of the day there is something about the creative process of any artist that cannot be verbalized.

That's certainly true, because if you could truly verbalize it, you wouldn't have to do it architecturally.

You spoke earlier about your work as having narratives.

Architecture is a language balanced between meaning and silence. But unlike Wittgenstein, who thought that where there is silence there is nothing more to say, I believe, on the contrary, that where there is silence there is most to be said. I've never believed in the silent space of architecture where the forms create the illusion that all has been said. I prefer buildings that don't anesthetize us but make us more alive.

It seems that both the paradox and the glory of architecture is that it uses material to create nonmaterial experiences and to transcend them.

Transcending them would be virtual reality, but no matter what the fantasies, we can't live in a virtual world. So the materialism of architecture is a perfect reflection of ourselves. We are body and soul that cannot be separated except perhaps in death. For now, we have to deal with real materials.

One of the things that fascinates me about where your work is going now is that there are so many high-rise buildings, so many skyscrapers that are building types that are utterly different from museums in almost every way.

It's amazing. I have now more than two dozen skyscrapers in design or in construction. The population of the world is growing exponentially; the skyscraper is no longer an exception or a luxury, it fulfills new demands for sustainability. It's also the embodiment of dreams and aspirations—how to shape not only the horizontal but the vertical dimension?

How are your skyscrapers part of a tradition? What are the particular gestures and designs?

The humanistic tradition in architecture has been under a real attack, particularly by architects who think that "computer-aided" design has morphed into computer design. I try to think differently. How can these buildings, which are so technically advanced, become more human, have a more physiognomic relationship to the environment, become more a part of our communities? I try to stay away

from the simplistic idea of geometric projection where you take a plan and project it into an extruded form. In fact, my thought is just the opposite: How can I make each form as different, and as distinct, as possible? Each level of the city has a different meaning, so the skyscraper should reflect the vertical complexity of the city.

I notice in your assembly of towers and apartment blocks for the Reflections project in Singapore that you have done very elaborate gardens at the top and that the towers bend slightly.

Yes, the towers all bend. They're actually double-curved. This is an interesting story. Initially, I proposed the double curve to the client, and then we presented it to the authorities, and they really embraced it. The towers are much taller than the typical towers that have previously been built, because they bring the idea of the garden to the heights of Singapore. You can see it from Mount Faber, and you can really enjoy the new tropical vision. The double curve gives a unique view on the horizon; the promenade along the bay makes this complex, yet very pleasant, at the pedestrian level, which is important due to the density.

In working with the developers, as it often happens, you develop a design, and the developers bring economic pressure, and they

ask you to scale back your design. So I took away one of the curved sides and reconfigured the core. Then the planning commissioners asked us to present again. Their response was, That's not what we gave you permission to build. We want the double curve back. We understand the difficulty, but that's exactly what made it unique and harmonic, with the reflections of Keppel Bay. Our client agreed to go back to the original geometry. So now the series of double-curved buildings is under construction. They have very particular light. The light moves in a very particular way over and through the facade, and even with the subtleties the building is not a static one. Of course, it's a complex form to build. But the core is completely vertical, and the building itself makes the individual apartments unique, and the gestures toward Keppel Bay have an almost aquatic atmosphere.

And the gardens will be visible from a distance?

Highly. The gardens are many, many stories high and will be seen from large distances.

So those unable to access them will still have the luxury of seeing their beauty.

People will be able to look at these gardens in the sky and see the beautiful foliage. To create a sustainable building, to create an image of a sustainable building, is not just in words. It should actually be a physical part.

Did this emerge out of the idea that you began to explore with the original Freedom Tower?

Certainly, initially. In Singapore, I had the chance to really explore this idea with a client who wanted to raise the bar. There are over 1,200 apartments, and with the double curve, the units shift around the core. It's not just interesting from the outside; internally, it offers a new way to experience the bay.

That brings to mind, for me, the condominiums in Denver.

The DAM Residences are very unusual. They're very disciplined units, single-loaded because they wrap around the parking garage. Every unit has been shaped distinctly. Even though there are two rectilinear buildings, each unit takes advantage of its position within the block.

To my knowledge, this housing project is the only one in which every unit within a block is uniquely shaped. There is not a single apartment plan that is a repetition of some-one else's. Each home has a unique layout and sense of light and space.

Yes. Was Denver your first residential project?

Actually it's the second—my first is hous-ing for the elderly, which is right now under construction in Brunnen at the entrance to Bern, the capital of Switzerland. The housing was designed as part of a mixed-use project. It's an unusual complex spanning the highway that incorporates the usual mix of cinemas, food courts, and department stores but also a hotel and a spectacular wellness and spa center. It's a great environment for senior citizens with its accessibility to entertain-ment, shopping, restaurants, fitness, and spa. What is perhaps the most exciting thing for me architecturally is that I have been able to build public spaces in the mall and shape the wellness facilities as dramatically as any of the museum spaces I have designed. And the entire complex breaks the form of large vol-umes with its wooden cladding and becomes a center of a new neighborhood that other-wise would have been the typical periphery condition.

The Ascent in Covington, Kentucky, is another unusual condominium on an unusual site.

The building is at the foot of the Roebling Bridge on the Ohio River. The curvature of the Ascent, the curvature of the cables of the bridge, the reflections and subtleties of water on the river as it moves across the site, the shimmering of the building as the light reflects off the facade: all were very, very strongly influenced by the site. The building is almost like topography. At its low point, it's about twelve or thirteen stories, and then it rises to twenty-two stories. The Ascent contributes to the reawakening of the urban potential of the greater Cincinnati area, and it does it for almost the same amount of construction bud-get as the most typical box!

And that's something that has struck me many times when I've been thinking of residential work, that often civic buildings, museums and so on, are celebrated, but actually it is equally important to judge cities by the way people live in them. That's why we love Paris or New York or London, cities that have a great history of dwelling. And I think contributing to that history is as important as contributing to our civic history.

That's a wonderful point actually. We think of Paris, New York, London, in terms of the dwell-ing places as much as in terms of the monu-ments. When you picture Park Avenue, whether or not you like those buildings, that's what you picture, that row of apartments.

Exactly. I think the twenty-first century will have more emphasis on how people live. Housing is becoming the foreground in cities, and I think that's a good trend, particularly in a democratic society where people's lives are celebrated rather than those of dictators or monarchs.

While we're still on the subject of tall buildings, let's talk about L Tower in Toronto.

The combination of programs is very unusual. The base of the building embraces an existing theater with loading docks. The ground levels become a cultural facility—the first six floors are delegated as art labs. On the street level, there will be a lively piazza and public space in a very important part of Toronto, which certainly needs more enlivened open space.

I shaped this large-scale building so its top would not cast shadows on an adjacent park. The building looks kind of whimsical maybe, and even slightly melodious, but actually the curve is adjusted in three dimensions to accommodate the unusual site. And by doing so, the building has acquired a specific and unusual profile that makes it distinctly related to its *genius loci*.

Let's talk a little bit about your building in Warsaw.

The site for Zlota 44 in Warsaw was familiar to me because I grew up in postwar Poland. The Palace of Culture—that oppressive gift of Stalin—is just across the street. For me, it always cast the shadow of Communism over the city. I decided that the design had to address this particular condition. Zlota 44 brings back the sweep of the Polish eagle, which penetrates the entire building. It's a display of optimism and a celebration of the beauty of Warsaw.

Warsaw really needs more people living in the center. Building a high-rise residential tower is not just an economic idea; it's also a sustainable idea. Zlota 44 has been designed to the optimum level of sustainability. Bringing people back to the center and promoting urban life is equally important. And coincidentally, it is just meters away from where my mother lived with her large Hasidic family. It's almost as if I've come full circle in my life with this project.

Talking about full circle, you're building a huge project in Milan, a city where you also used to live.

It's very exciting to build in cities where I've lived—New York, Warsaw, Milan, Berlin, London,

Tel Aviv, and Toronto. These are all places I've lived in, and when you come back in another capacity, you can harness your love for a city in a different way. And I love Milan. Our daughter was born there and my sons went to school there and still speak fluent Italian to each other!

As the master planner of the old fairgrounds, I thought to introduce a huge central park. Milan is, of course, well known for its great architecture, but like most cities, it needs more green space. The site is sixty-four acres, four times the size of Ground Zero. My strategy was to give each of the architects, Zaha Hadid, Arata Isozaki, Pier Paolo Maggiora, and myself, a mix of housing, high-rise, retail, and culture, a mix of architectural possibilities, and in that way to diversify the site with different architectural individualities. Site preparation has already started, and I'm just finishing the construction drawings for my part of the housing and working on design development for the tower and the museum.

Since cities are in global competition today, it's a great opportunity to connect innovation with tradition. Buildings have always been a means of communicating a new significance to a place and a new significance to people's perception of that place. Sometimes I feel that even a small building, if it's well thought out, if it's cared for, if it's handled with a certain love, has an impact beyond its size.

Well, your building in Hong Kong is not small but it certainly has a pretty big visual impact. Let's talk about that.

I am designing a media center for the City University of Hong Kong. Hong Kong is known for its great office buildings. This school building will bring cultural expression to Kowloon. The building is very compact and efficient with thousands of square meters of animation laboratories, sound stages, classrooms, and lecture halls. I wanted the design to embody the ambition and energy of the media school within the fastest growing university in

Hong Kong and to turn an educational building into an icon.

Let's go back to shopping centers for a minute. I'm fascinated that you're building in Las Vegas.

MGM Mirage, our client, had a very bold idea. They didn't want imitative architecture; they wanted an entirely new symbol for the vast city center site. Las Vegas has become a city that requires architecture. And I believe that what our client has asked for is a fundamental shift from what's currently there. And like the galleria in Milan, which is from the nineteenth century, this is the galleria of the twenty-first century. I asked myself what the flaneur, the urban poet, would do today. What would he go to see? Where would he meet his friends, have dinner, coffee, a drink? I tried to create an environment of wonder and amazement. People can even see the real sky! I think that CityCenter, right on the Strip, will have a great impact on proving Las Vegas to be a metropolis in the making. The retail and entertainment space is like a knot that ties together hotels, casinos, and residential blocks and thus is visible in the round. That's why I designed the roof as a landscape in itself. And it is a LEED project.

It is remarkable to see that the Strip has sort of developed an urbanism in spite of itself. At night people just walk there, one place to the next, and the streets are thronged.

Is it so different from ancient Rome? In Rome, when you look at the Colosseum, when you look at all the entertainment, you realize it became a city because there was a desire to be there for many different reasons. There is something fantastic about Las Vegas: it's not the caricature that many people have of it. The city is growing by thousands of people every week. It needs a new city center, a sophisticated, urban place that will be attractive to families, to kids, and of course to visitors. It needs contemporary architecture rather than illusionistic buildings.

It's fascinating to think of how the early Las Vegas, the primitive Las Vegas, was an original creation. And then as it grew, it took refuge in historicism and nostalgia. Now it is returning to being an original creation.

Architecture should always strive to be original!

You are known for so many large-scale projects. What about the other end of the architectural spectrum—private homes?

I recently designed a house in Connecticut, now under construction, for two art lovers. These extraordinary clients have impeccable taste and expertise in architecture. I designed an intimate house nestled in the landscape. All the planes continually turn in different directions, and this choreography creates a fusion of atmospheres that redefine the notion of enclosure. It's clad in dark reflective stainless steel. The house grows from the inside and is expressed with the purity of non-Cartesian geometry.

The challenge is so interesting, of course.

I'm also designing a prefabricated, passive-energy house that will feel like a unique villa. The cladding, for example, uses new ecological technologies, and the house will produce more energy than it consumes. The pieces are fabricated so that they can be transported on a flatbed truck and easily assembled. And of course, the cost has to be in the frame of the marketplace.

Is there any type of building that you have not yet had an opportunity to do that you very much want to do?

Sure, there are buildings I would love to build— a synagogue, a church, a mosque. And even an airport—since I spend so much time in them.

Ground Zero brought you back to New York from Berlin. Besides that project you have a very large residential tower in New York.

I'm excited to be building a totally innovative tower close to the Flatiron Building in a historically interesting area of New York. The building doesn't occupy a new footprint but threads itself in a delicate way through an existing structure. At the same time it aspires to contribute to the composition of New York City's streetscape and skyline. It has a new idea of permeability and outdoor space. It's next to the MetLife Tower so it has to be iconic not by choice but by necessity!

Your architecture is visible wherever it is.

Well, I've never understood the notion of neutral architecture. Everything speaks to you. Some buildings sing and others simply tell you that they have nothing to say.

Neutral architecture is sort of like neutral music.

Yes. It's the Muzak of architecture. It's not a value that I ever aspired to. One should take a position in this life, even if it is sometimes controversial. Life is about passions and emotions that enrich experience, not about the coolness of architectural fashion.

Is this a great moment for architecture, do you think?

I think it's an incredible moment, not just for our studio, but in general. When I think back to my days as a student, I had great teachers, but architecture was very limited. Architecture in school was far more exciting and interesting than architectural practice. Now, architecture is so incredibly dynamic and innovative that it has surpassed academia.

It's an amazing period of rediscovery; architecture suddenly has taken off. It's because people, of all walks of life, are interested in it, not just people around a table in a board room. The public has become involved and engaged and much more knowledgeable. Ground Zero and the importance of that competition signified a global change. People now care about their cities a lot more vocally. The destruction of 9/11 was horrifying, but people came together and took the time to personalize a process that had become all too depersonalized.

So in a way, what you're saying is that the impact of Ground Zero on the architectural culture will affect things beyond Ground Zero itself.

I think the great thing about democracy is that participation is not just some abstraction. As Winston Churchill pointed out, democracy despite all its flaws is the best of all systems. It's something I experience every day.

The Jewish Museum Berlin has become one of the most potent Holocaust memorials in the world even though that was not its central reason for being. It has become so, and it has been so widely admired that it has been a powerful force in the transformation of Berlin.

I DID SOMETHING I BELIEVED IN, WHICH WAS TO TRANSFORM THE ENTIRE STRUC- TURE INTO A DISCOURSE ABOUT GERMAN- JEWISH HISTORY.

THE JEWISH
MUSEUM
THEMATIZES
AND INTE-
GRATES, FOR
THE FIRST TIME
IN POSTWAR
GERMANY, THE
HISTORY OF
THE JEWS IN
GERMANY AND
THE REPERCUS-
SIONS OF THE
HOLOCAUST.
ORIGINALLY A
DEPARTMENT
OF THE BERLIN
MUSEUM, IT HAS
BECOME AN
INDEPENDENT
INSTITUTION.

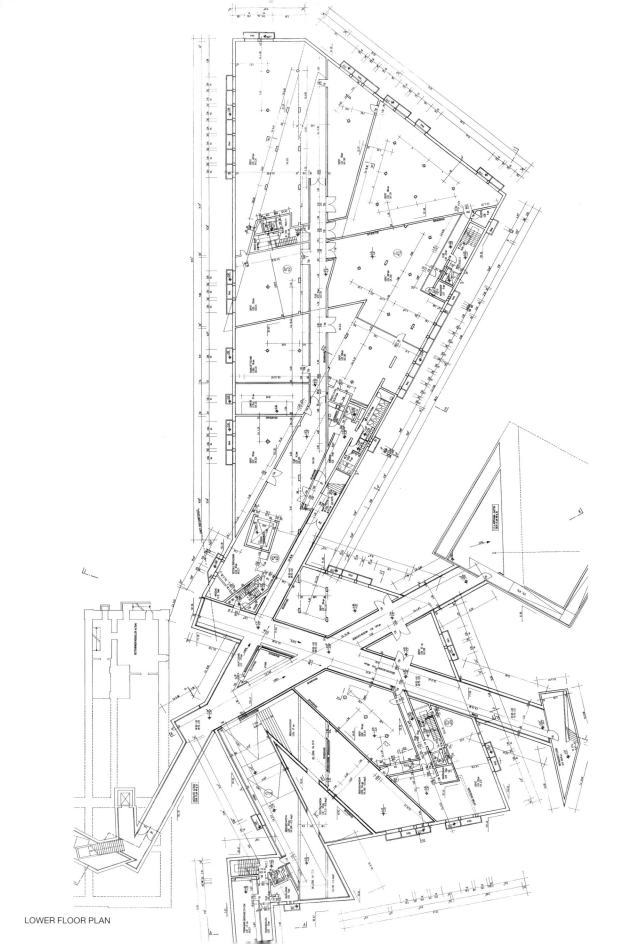

LOWER FLOOR PLAN

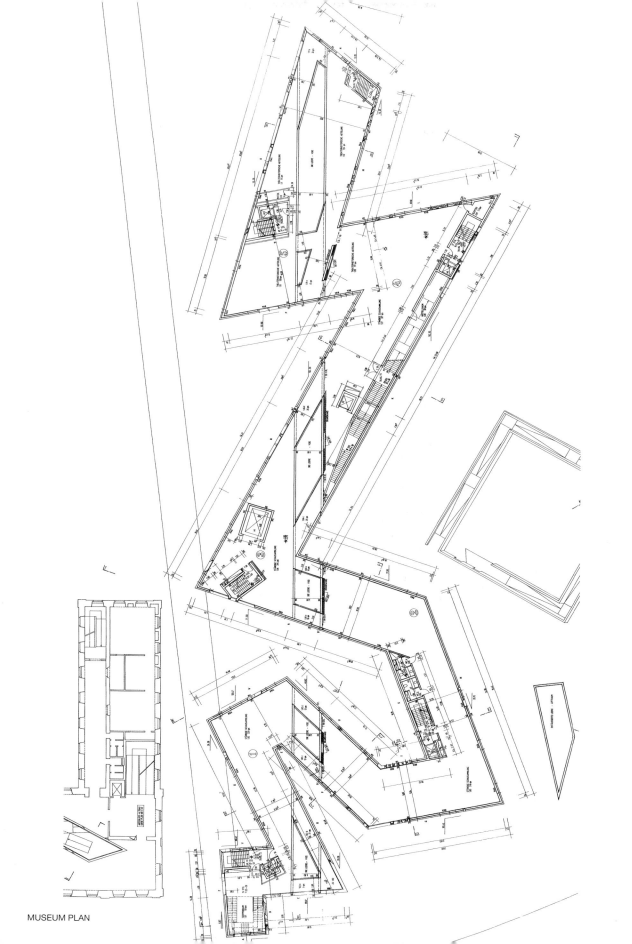

MUSEUM PLAN

THE JEWISH
MUSEUM
BERLIN STANDS
NEXT TO THE
ORIGINAL
BUILDING OF
THE BERLIN
MUSEUM,
THE FORMER
COLLEGIEN-
HAUS. THE
BAROQUE
BUILDING WAS
DESIGNED
BY PHILIP
GERLACH IN
1735.

THE ZINC EXTERIOR IS INCISED WITH LINES THAT REFER TO THE STAR OF DAVID. THE POSITIONING OF THE WINDOWS FOLLOWS A MATRIX THAT EXPRESSES THE LINK BETWEEN JEWISH TRADITION AND GERMAN CULTURE BY PLOTTING THE ADDRESSES OF PROMINENT JEWISH AND GERMAN CITIZENS ON A MAP OF PREWAR BERLIN.

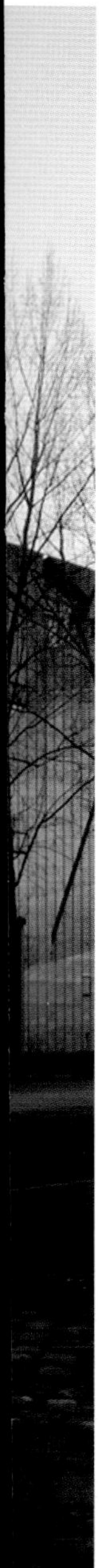

THE
HOLOCAUST
TOWER AND
THE GARDEN
OF EXILE ARE
ELEMENTS IN
THE OVERALL
COMPOSITION
OF THE JEWISH
MUSEUM.

THE HOLOCAUST
TOWER IS LIT
BY A SINGLE
NARROW SLIT
HIGH ABOVE THE
GROUND.

CUTTING THROUGH THE MUSEUM IS THE VOID, AROUND WHICH THE EXHIBITIONS ARE ORGANIZED. SIXTY THRESHOLDS BRIDGE THE VOID. IN THE MEMORY VOID IS THE INSTALLATION *SHALECHET* (*FALLEN LEAVES*) BY MENASHE KADISHMAN.

THREE UNDER-
GROUND
"ROADS"
SYMBOLIZE
THREE PATHS
IN THE HISTORY
OF GERMAN
JEWS. THE
FIRST LEADS
TO THE DEAD
END OF THE
HOLOCAUST
TOWER, THE
SECOND TO
THE GARDEN
OF EXILE, AND
THE THIRD TO
THE STAIR OF
CONTINU-
ITY AND
EXHIBITIONS.

THE AXIS OF
CONTINUITY,
AND THE MAIN
STAIR, REP-
RESENT THE
CONTINUATION
OF BERLIN'S
HISTORY.

ILLUMINATING
THE EXHIBITION
SPACES ARE
WINDOWS THAT
ARE PART OF
THE STAR OF
DAVID MATRIX
IMPRINTED ON
THE BUILDING.

THE GARDEN OF EXILE REPRESENTS THE EXILE AND EMIGRATION OF JEWS FROM GERMANY.

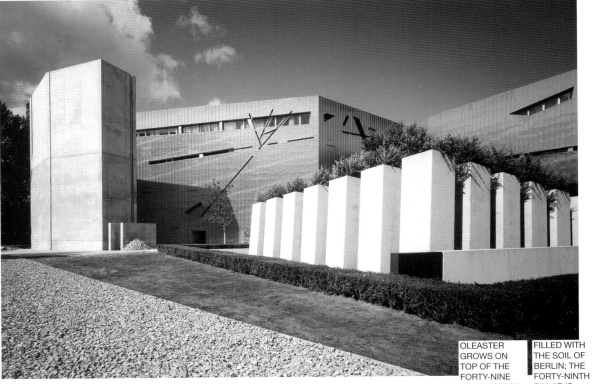

OLEASTER GROWS ON TOP OF THE FORTY-NINE CONCRETE PILLARS. FORTY-EIGHT PILLARS, REPRESENTING THE BIRTH OF ISRAEL, ARE FILLED WITH THE SOIL OF BERLIN; THE FORTY-NINTH PILLAR IS FILLED WITH THE SOIL OF ISRAEL.

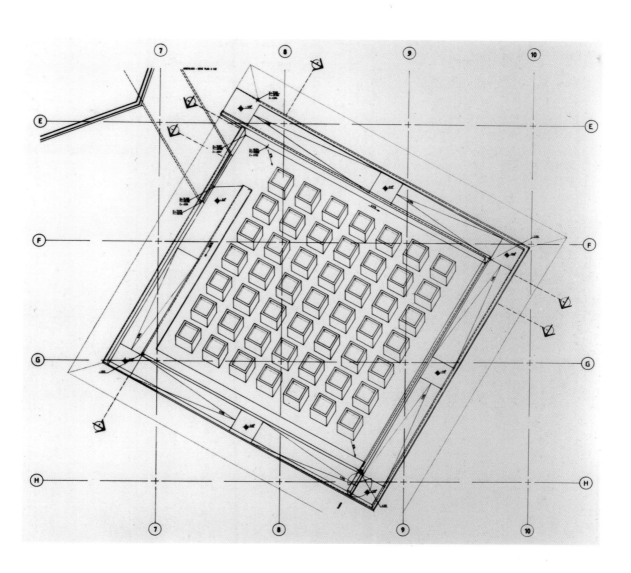

PLAN, GARDEN
OF EXILE

THE GLASS COURTYARD, COMPLETED IN 2007, SPANS THE WINGS OF THE COLLEGIEN-HAUS. IT EXTENDS THE LOBBY AND PROVIDES SPACE FOR SPECIAL EVENTS, LECTURES, CONCERTS, AND DINNERS.

THE ROOF OF THE COURTYARD IS SUPPORTED BY FOUR FREE-STANDING BUNDLES OF STEEL PILLARS THAT RESEMBLE THE STRUCTURE OF A TREE.

How do you approach the skyscraper, how do you find form for it,
how do you feel your towers either fit in or do not fit in to the
history of the skyscraper as we've known it thus far?

I DON'T USE A DIFFERENT METHOD TO DESIGN A SKY— SCRAPER THAN I WOULD USE FOR A MUSEUM.

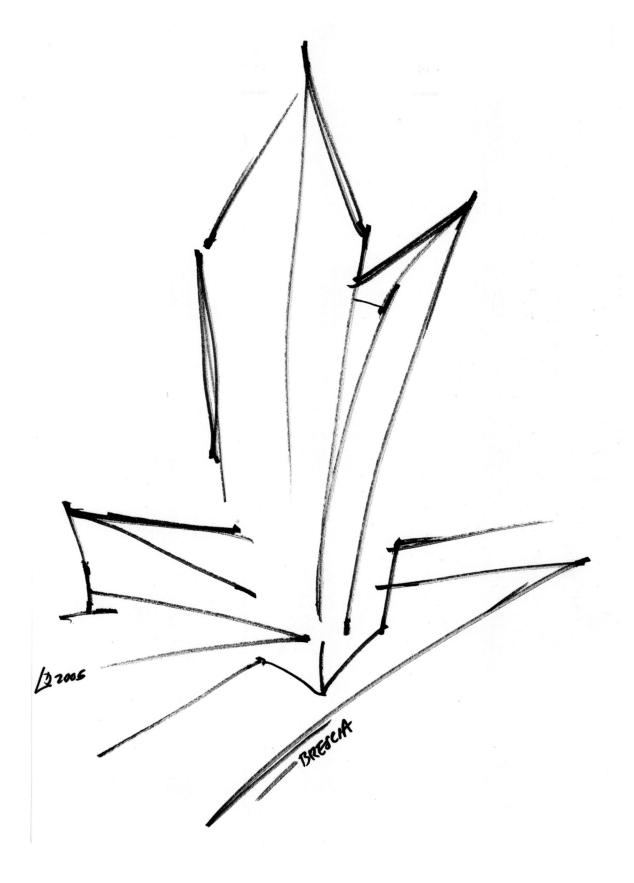

THE SOFT AND
TRANSPARENT
SURFACE OF
THE BUILDING
IS COMPOSED
OF A DOUBLE
LAYER OF
GLASS. EVER
CHANGING
IN ITS ARTICU-
LATION, IT
RESPONDS TO
THE UNIQUE
QUALITIES
OF LIGHT IN
BRESCIA.

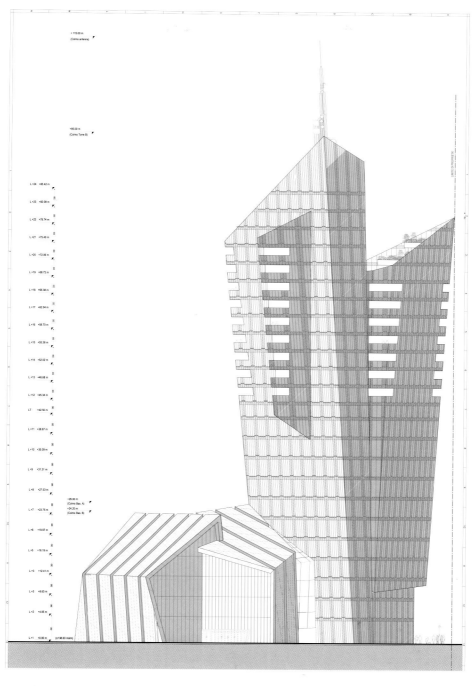

+ 115.00 m
(Colmo antenna)

+95.00 m
(Colmo Torre B)

L +24 +85.42 m
L +23 +82.08 m
L +22 +78.74 m
L +21 +75.40 m
L +20 +72.06 m
L +19 +68.72 m
L +18 +65.38 m
L +17 +62.04 m
L +16 +58.70 m
L +15 +55.36 m
L +14 +52.02 m
L +13 +48.68 m
L +12 +45.34 m
LT   +42.50 m
L +11 +38.87 m
L +10 +35.09 m
L +9   +31.31 m
L +8   +27.53 m
                          +26.00 m
                          (Colmo Bas. A)
L +7   +23.75 m   +24.20 m
                          (Colmo Bas. B)
L +6   +19.97 m
L +5   +16.19 m
L +3   +12.41 m
L +3   +8.63 m
L +2   +4.85 m
L +1   +0.00 m (±138.63 mslm)

SOUTH
ELEVATION

14.D 160.2 mq

TYPICAL
OFFICE PLAN

14.A 169.0 mq

14.E 201.9

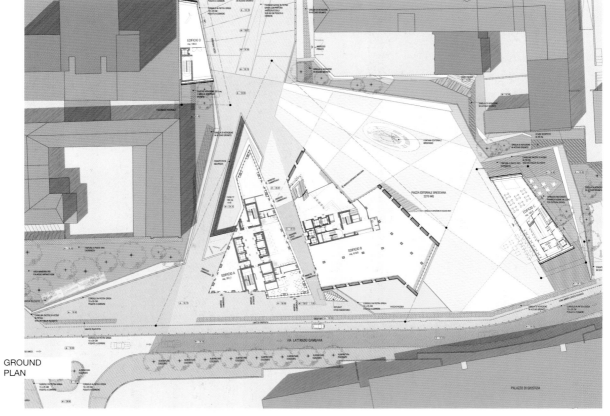

GROUND
PLAN

THE TOWER
MIXES OFFICE
AND RESIDEN-
TIAL USES. THE
CANTED WALLS
OPEN UPWARD.

It's interesting that an architect like you would design a shopping and leisure center in Switzerland.

I WAS INSPIRED BY THE MARX BROTHERS' FILM *THE BIG STORE*, WHICH AFFIRMS THAT LIFE IS THE UNEXPECTED CROSSROADS OF POSSIBILITIES.

THE SHOPPING AND LEISURE CENTER, WHICH SPANS THE HIGHWAY, CREATES A GATEWAY INTO BERN AND HAS ITS OWN HIGHWAY EXIT, TRAM, AND TRAIN STATION.

THE EXTERIOR MATERIAL OF THE COMPLEX IS ACACIA WOOD. THIS ENVIRON-MENTALLY RESPONSIBLE MATERIAL, NOT OFTEN FOUND ALONG A HIGHWAY, HARMONIZES WITH THE LANDSCAPE.

THE ARRIVAL
PLAZA IS
FRAMED BY
A VERTICAL
HOTEL AND
HORIZON-
TAL SENIOR
RESIDENCES.
THE OBLIQUE
OPENINGS OF
THE SHOPPING
CENTER ILLU-
MINATE THE
BUILDING DAY
AND NIGHT.

THE PLAY OF
ARCHITEC-
TURAL SPACE
ECHOES
THE FUN OF
SWIMMING
AND WATER
SPORTS.

THE INTERSEC-
TION OF SHOP-
PING ACTIVITY
AND COMPLEX
FORMS BRINGS
THE PUBLIC
SPACE TO LIFE.

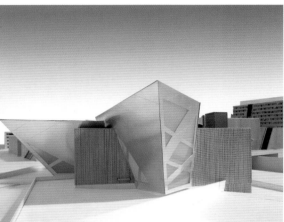

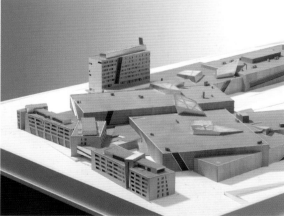

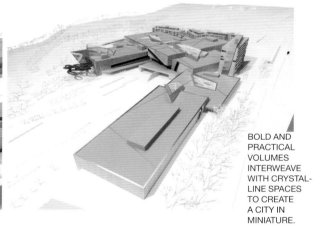

BOLD AND
PRACTICAL
VOLUMES
INTERWEAVE
WITH CRYSTAL-
LINE SPACES
TO CREATE
A CITY IN
MINIATURE.

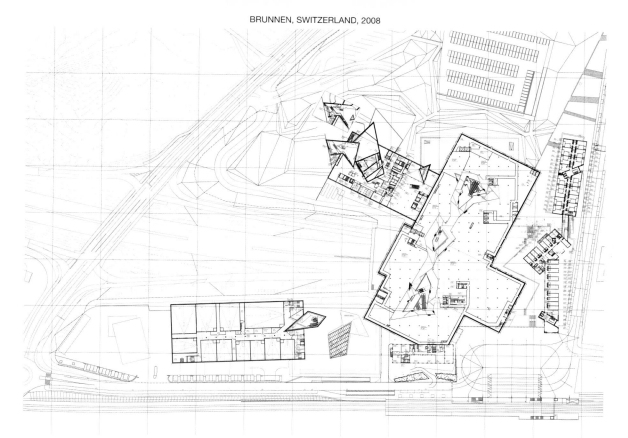

UPPER
FLOOR PLAN

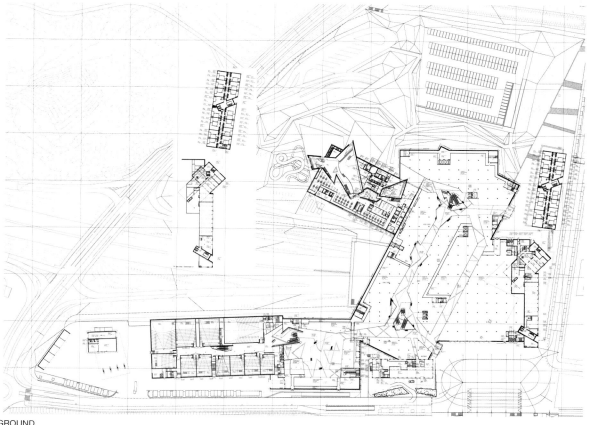

GROUND
PLAN

Long ago, someone asked Louis Kahn if he preferred the kind of clients who came to him knowing exactly what they wanted or the clients who didn't have any idea what they wanted and left it all up to him. And he said, Neither of those is the kind of client I want. I want the kind of client who knows what he aspires to.

I APPRECIATE A CLIENT WHO QUESTIONS THE ASPIRATIONS OF THE PAST AND IS READY TO FORGE THE FUTURE.

HIGH-DENSITY RESIDENTIAL TOWERS, HOTEL, AND OFFICES ARE CAREFULLY POSITIONED ON THE BUSAN WATERFRONT TO CREATE A PARK AND A PROMENADE.

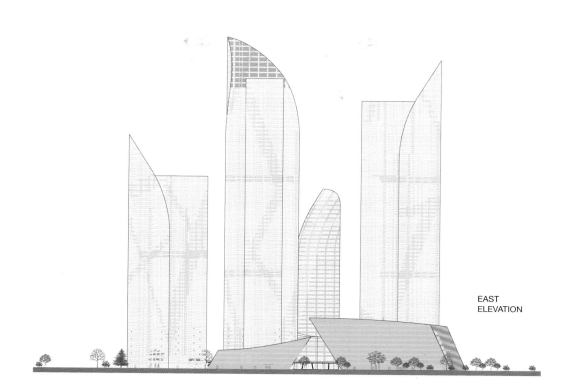

EAST
ELEVATION

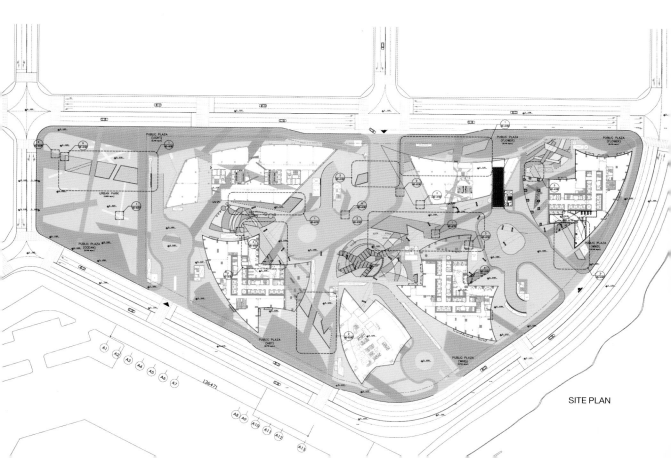

SITE PLAN

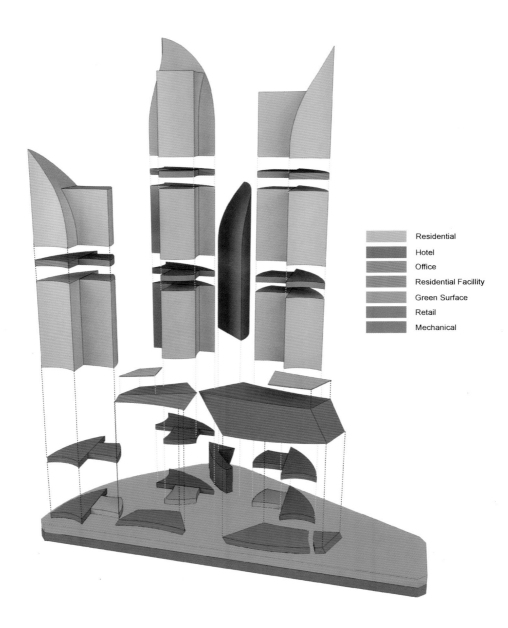

Residential
Hotel
Office
Residential Facillity
Green Surface
Retail
Mechanical

THE FORMS ARE SCULPTED TO EXPRESS THE POWER OF OCEAN WAVES, THE GRACEFUL SHAPES OF SAILS ON THE WATER, AND THE ELEGANT CURVES OF TRADITIONAL KOREAN ARCHITECTURE.

THE VARIED
HEIGHTS OF
THE INDIVIDUAL
BUILDINGS
AND THE
SUBTLE PLAY
OF CURVES
CREATE A
SCULPTURAL
COMPOSI-
TION ON THE
HORIZON.

THE TOWERS RING A LANDSCAPED PARK THAT PROVIDES OPEN SPACE FOR RESIDENTS, VISITORS, AND THOSE WHO LIVE IN BUSAN.

The Danish Jewish Museum is another museum dealing with
Jewish history. What drew you to this project?

THE ACT OF SAVING DANISH JEWS FROM THE HOLOCAUST WAS A LIGHT IN THE DARKNESS OF THOSE TIMES.

THE DESIGN OF THE DANISH JEWISH MUSEUM WAS INSPIRED BY THE MASS RESCUE OF ROUGHLY EIGHT THOU-SAND JEWS IN OCTOBER 1943 BY THEIR COM-PATRIOTS. THE HEBREW WORD *MITZVAH*—AN OBLIGATION OR GOOD DEED— IS SYMBOLIZED IN THE FORM AND STRUC-TURE OF THE MUSEUM.

THE SMALL DOOR TO THE MUSEUM OPENS OFF AN INTIMATE PUBLIC PLAZA.

FOUR INTERSECTING PLANES STRUCTURE THE INTERIOR LANDSCAPE. THE FOUR PLANES— EXODUS, WILDERNESS, THE GIVING OF THE LAW, AND THE PROMISED LAND—ARE ARTICULATED IN THE CORRUGATED FLOOR SECTIONS, IN THE PROJECTION OF WALLS AND VITRINES, AND IN THE PATH OF THE INSTALLATION.

PLAN

ANCIENT BRICK
WALLS, VEC-
TORS OF LIGHT,
FRAGMENTS
OF MEMORY
INTERSECT IN
THE EXHIBITION
SPACE.

THE SLOPING WOODEN FLOOR AND THE CARVED WOODEN INTERIOR RECALL THE BOATS THAT TRANSPORTED THE DANISH JEWS TO SAFETY.

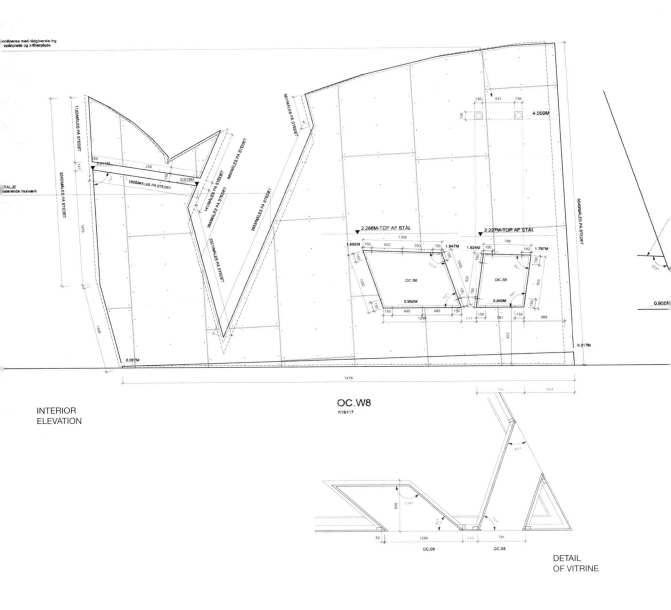

INTERIOR
ELEVATION

OC.W8
K13/117

DETAIL
OF VITRINE

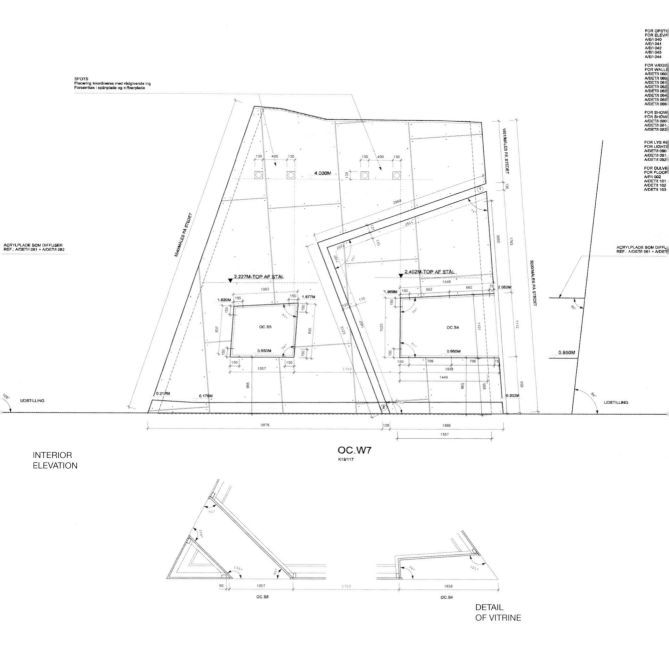

INTERIOR
ELEVATION

OC.W7
K13/117

DETAIL
OF VITRINE

Your residential project in Kentucky is an unusual condominium on an unusual site. Opposite the Roebling Bridge, it faces downtown Cincinnati across the river. How do the bridge and that site influence your design?

I WANTED A BUILDING WITH A SENSE OF MOVEMENT, COLOR, AND FORM THAT IS EVOCATIVE OF THE RIVER AND THE BRIDGE.

THE BUILDING'S
EMPHATIC
UPWARD SWEEP
IS A SYMBOL ON
THE HORIZON.

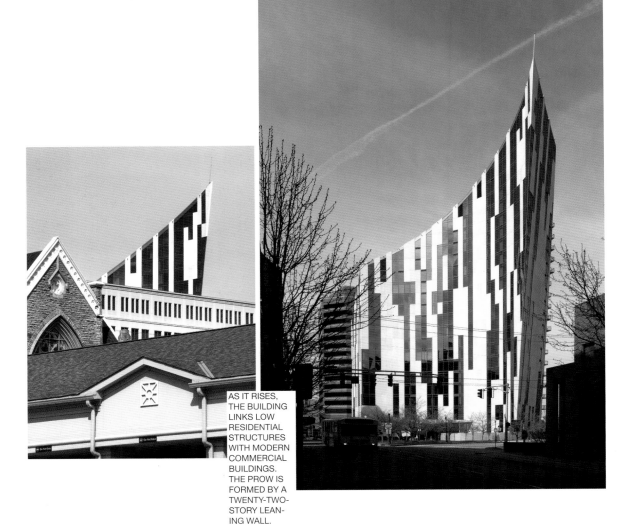

AS IT RISES, THE BUILDING LINKS LOW RESIDENTIAL STRUCTURES WITH MODERN COMMERCIAL BUILDINGS. THE PROW IS FORMED BY A TWENTY-TWO-STORY LEANING WALL.

THE ASCENT IS A GATEWAY TO THE ROEBLING BRIDGE OVER THE OHIO RIVER.

THE BUILDING
REDEFINES THE
WATER'S EDGE.

UNIT 02
1 BEDROOM FLAT + OFFICE
REPEATS ON FLOORS 02-09
1,246 SF

UNIT 03
2 BEDROOM FLAT
REPEATS ON FLOORS 02-11
2,195 SF

UNIT 01
2 BEDROOM FLAT
REPEATS ON FLOORS 02-09
1,960 SF

UNIT 04
2 BEDROOM FLAT
REPEATS ON FLOORS 02-14
2,266SF

UNIT 05
1 BEDROOM FLAT
REPEATS ON FLOORS 02-16
1000 SF

UNIT 06
2 BEDROOM FLAT
2,000 SF (at level 06)

LIVING
M BR
LIVING
DINING
M BR
DINING
BR 2
LIVING
OFFICE
DINING
DINING
LIVING
BR 2
OFFICE
M BR
LIVING
OFFICE
M BR
DINING
BR 2
M BR
LIVING
BR 2
DINING
BR 2
M BR

TYPICAL
FLOOR PLAN

You have spoken about the Rocky Mountains as being a portion of the inspiration for Denver. Is it that sort of external, physical thing or was it also something more conceptual?

I SAW TWO LINES GOING FOR A WALK IN DENVER, THE LINE OF THE ROCKIES AND THE LINE OF CULTURE. THEY MEET AND FORM THE MUSEUM ITSELF.

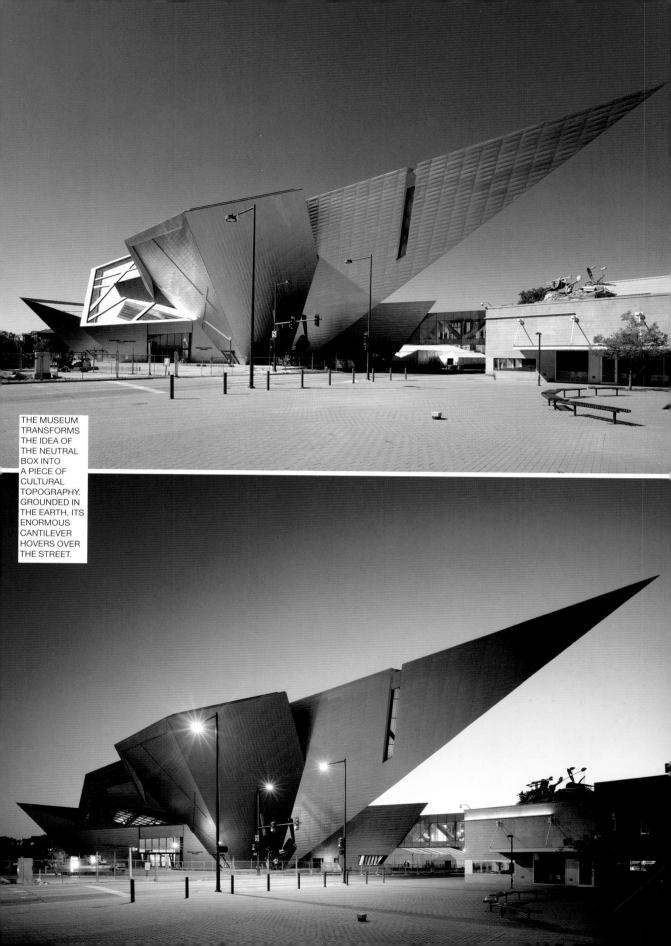

THE MUSEUM
TRANSFORMS
THE IDEA OF
THE NEUTRAL
BOX INTO
A PIECE OF
CULTURAL
TOPOGRAPHY.
GROUNDED IN
THE EARTH, ITS
ENORMOUS
CANTILEVER
HOVERS OVER
THE STREET.

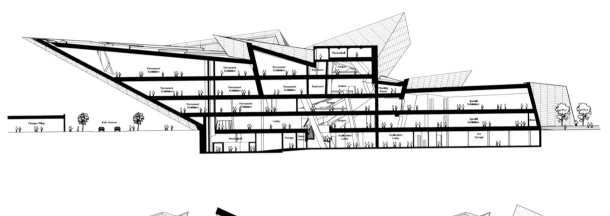

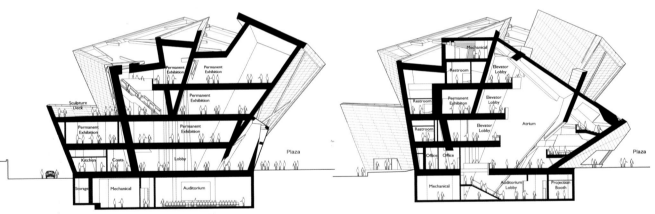

SECTIONS

THE VITALITY AND GROWTH OF THE CITY OF DENVER COUPLED WITH THE MAGNIFICENT LANDSCAPE OF THE ROCKY MOUNTAINS INSPIRES THE FORM OF THE NEW BUILDING FOR THE DENVER ART MUSEUM.

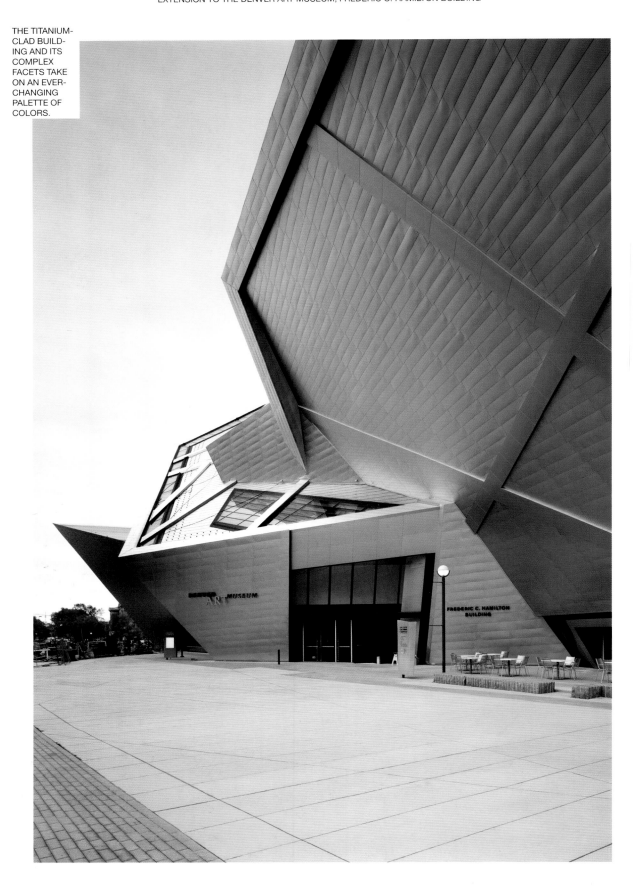

THE TITANIUM-
CLAD BUILD-
ING AND ITS
COMPLEX
FACETS TAKE
ON AN EVER-
CHANGING
PALETTE OF
COLORS.

THE CENTRAL ATRIUM, MAIN STAIR, AND SURROUND-ING PUBLIC SPACES SUGGEST THE ROCKIES AND THEIR VERTIGINOUS PERSPECTIVES.

THE CIRCU-
LAR DIGITAL
COUNTERS
IN THE MAIN
STAIRCASE ARE
PART OF *ENGI*,
AN INSTALLA-
TION BY TATSUO
MIYAJIMA.

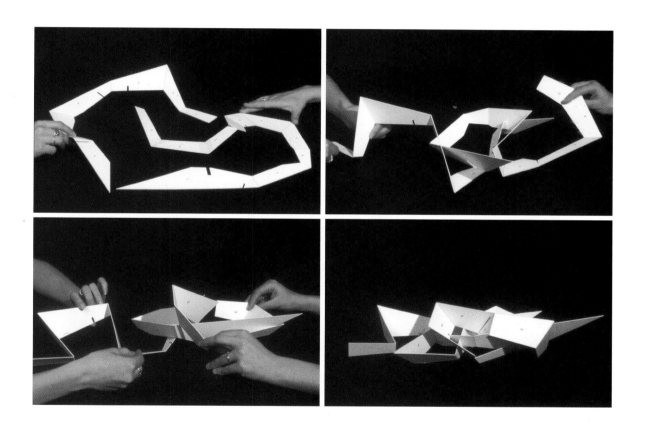

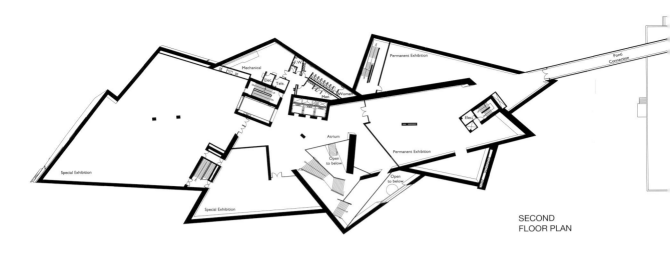

SECOND
FLOOR PLAN

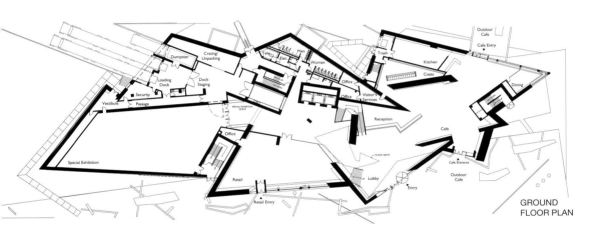

GROUND
FLOOR PLAN

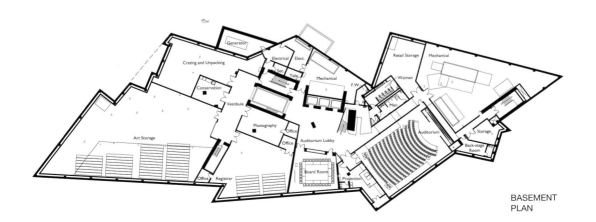

BASEMENT
PLAN

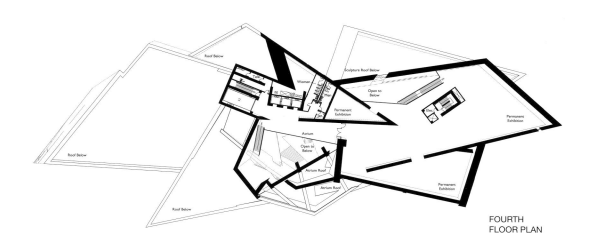

FOURTH
FLOOR PLAN

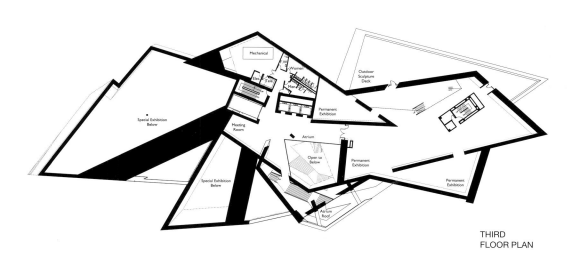

THIRD
FLOOR PLAN

ROCK FORMATION, BY JENNIFER STEINKAMP, IS A SITE-SPECIFIC DIGITAL VIDEO PROJECTION ON AN OBLIQUE WALL.

THE NATURE
OF THE NEW
GALLERIES
ADDRESSES
THE INDE-
TERMINATE
AND EVER-
SURPRISING
HORIZONS OF
CONTEMPO-
RARY ART.

LARGE FLEX-
IBLE VOLUMES
ACCOM-
MODATE THE
REQUIRE-
MENTS OF A
VARIETY OF
EXHIBITIONS.

ANTONY GORMLEY'S *QUANTUM CLOUD XXXIII* STANDS AT THE TIP.

The condominiums opposite the museum in Denver strike me as particularly exciting because you combine elements of the museum's aesthetic with more conventional space.

IT WAS A FANTAS-TIC OPPORTUNITY TO INVENT A MASTER PLAN, CIVIC SPACE, URBAN ART PLAZA, AND DIS-TINCTLY SHAPED APARTMENTS.

THE MUSEUM
RESIDENCES,
LIKE THE
DENVER ART
MUSEUM
ITSELF, ASPIRE
TO MAKE A
CULTURAL
NEXUS IN THE
CITY.

THE GLASS
AND ZINC
FACADES
CREATE A
KALEIDOSCOPE
OF LIGHT,
SHADOW,
AND TEXTURE
INSIDE THE
RESIDENCES.

EACH OF THE
MUSEUM
RESIDENCES
EXPRESSES ITS
PARTICULAR
LOCATION.

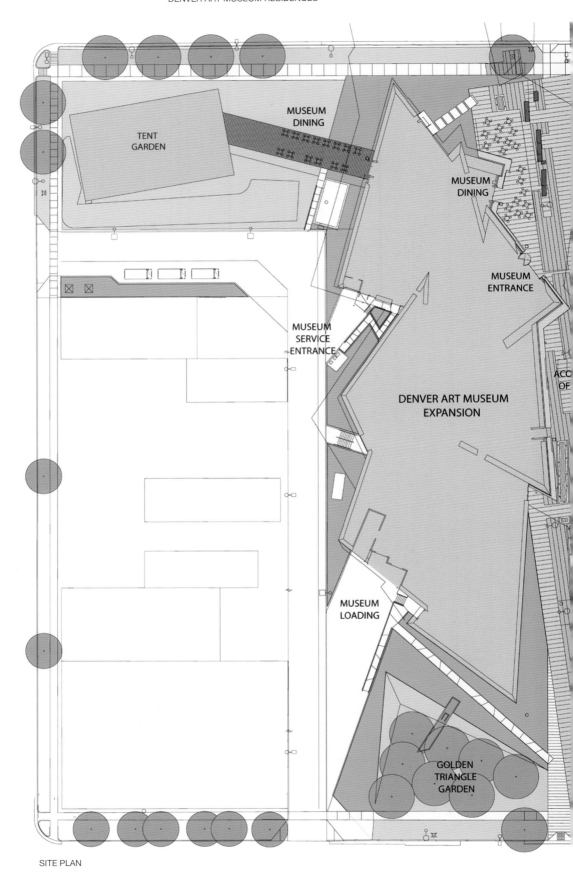

SITE PLAN

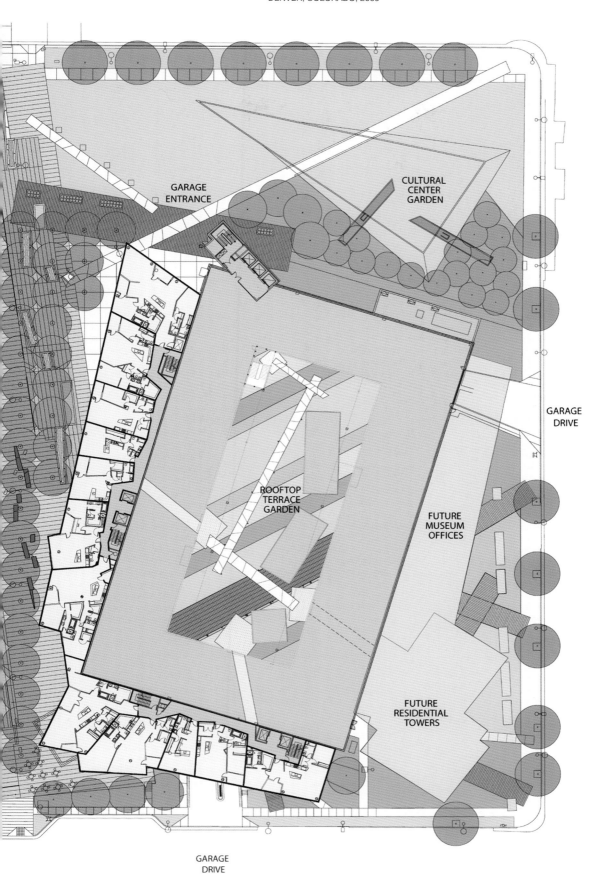

GARAGE
ENTRANCE

CULTURAL
CENTER
GARDEN

GARAGE
DRIVE

ROOFTOP
TERRACE
GARDEN

FUTURE
MUSEUM
OFFICES

FUTURE
RESIDENTIAL
TOWERS

GARAGE
DRIVE

THE MUSEUM
AND THE
MUSEUM
RESIDENCES
CONTRIBUTE
TO A NEW
CENTER FOR
DENVER.

The Military Museum in Dresden is behind historic walls.
How did you approach the design?

I BROKE THROUGH THE OLD WALLS IN ORDER TO SIGNAL A CHANGED VIEW OF THE MILITARY IN A DEMOCRATIC SOCIETY.

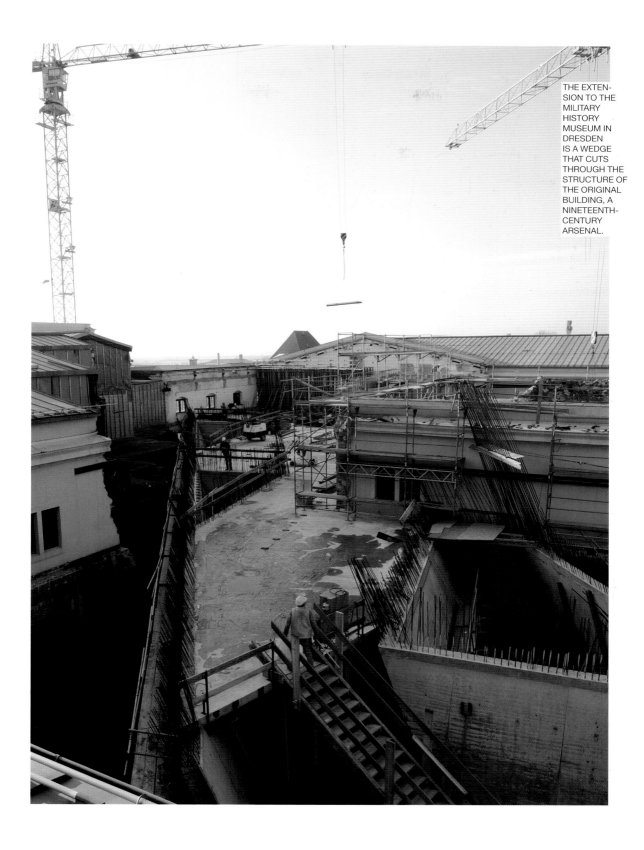

THE EXTEN-
SION TO THE
MILITARY
HISTORY
MUSEUM IN
DRESDEN
IS A WEDGE
THAT CUTS
THROUGH THE
STRUCTURE OF
THE ORIGINAL
BUILDING, A
NINETEENTH-
CENTURY
ARSENAL.

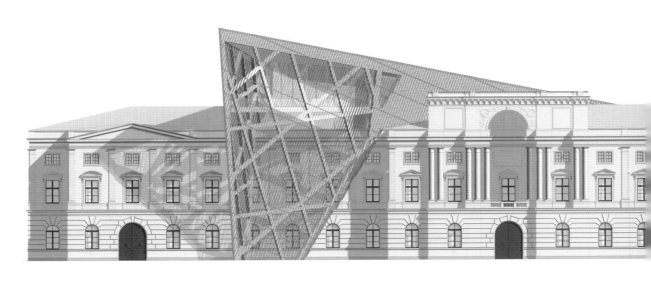

THE WEDGE SOARS ABOVE THE ROOF OF THE EXISTING BUILDING, OPENING IT TO THE HISTORIC CENTER OF DRESDEN.

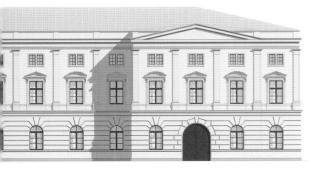

THE TRANS-
PARENT NEW
FACADE,
REFLECTING
THE OPENNESS
OF A DEMO-
CRATIC SOCI-
ETY, STANDS
AGAINST
THE OPACITY
OF THE OLD
FACADE.

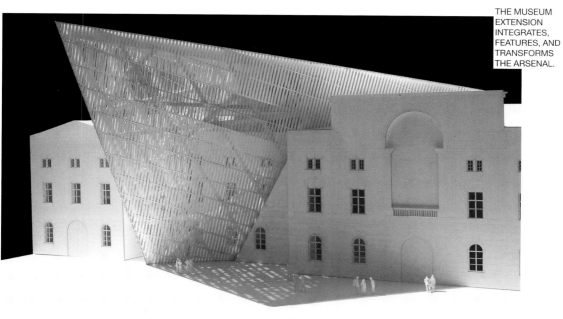

THE MUSEUM
EXTENSION
INTEGRATES,
FEATURES, AND
TRANSFORMS
THE ARSENAL.

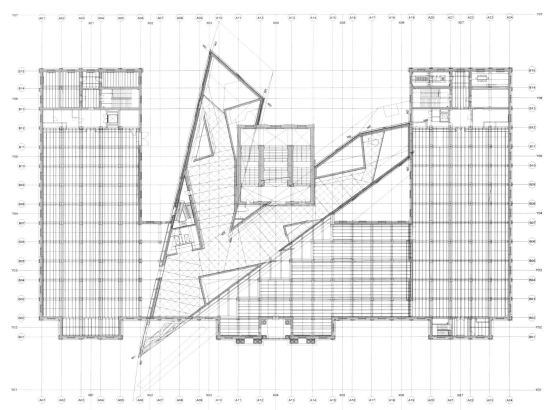

FIRST
FLOOR PLAN

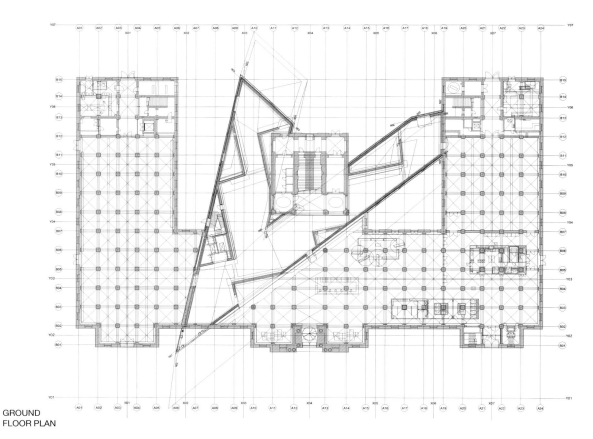

GROUND
FLOOR PLAN

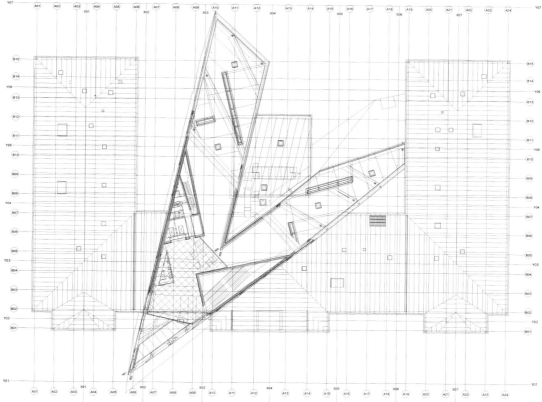

FIFTH
FLOOR PLAN

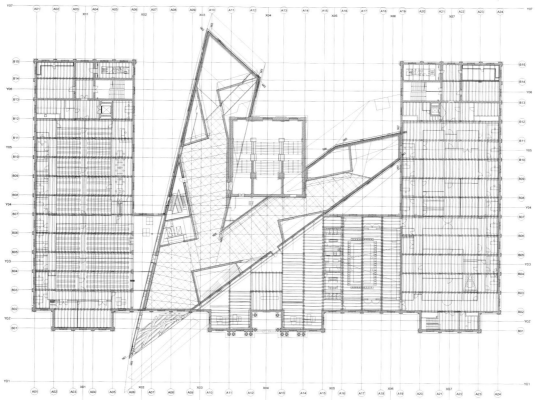

THIRD
FLOOR PLAN

SECTION

Hoehenkoten Altbau

Y01

B01   Y02   B

Fassadenabwicklung Neubau nach
Plaenen AFA_N001 bis AFA_N006

+30.42

OK.Traufe ca.+16.61

OK.F.FB+15.865

UK.F.DE. +15.095

95

OK.F.FB. +11,56

UK.F.DE. +10.93

Exedra

OK.F.FB. +6.51

OK.R.FB +6.45   OK.F.FB. ca.+6.5

SH.Tonne ca.+6.07

Tonnendecke

SH.Gewölbe +5,60 bis +5,67
SH.Joch +5.30 bis +5.37

SH.Bogen ca.+5.08

OK.Kapitell ca. +3.17

AAF
D500

AAF
D501

AIF
D581

Glas-Karusseltuer

Tor neu
0021.1/01
nach innen aufschlagend!
zu den Besucherzeiten immer
offenstehend! genaue Position
noch zu bestimmen !

Handlauf

OK.F.FB. ±0.00=141.79

OK. Gelaende gem. Fachplanung Aussenanlagen

OK.R.FB -0.36

Fundament Bestand
nach AM BAR 2004

Restlariofen Altbau

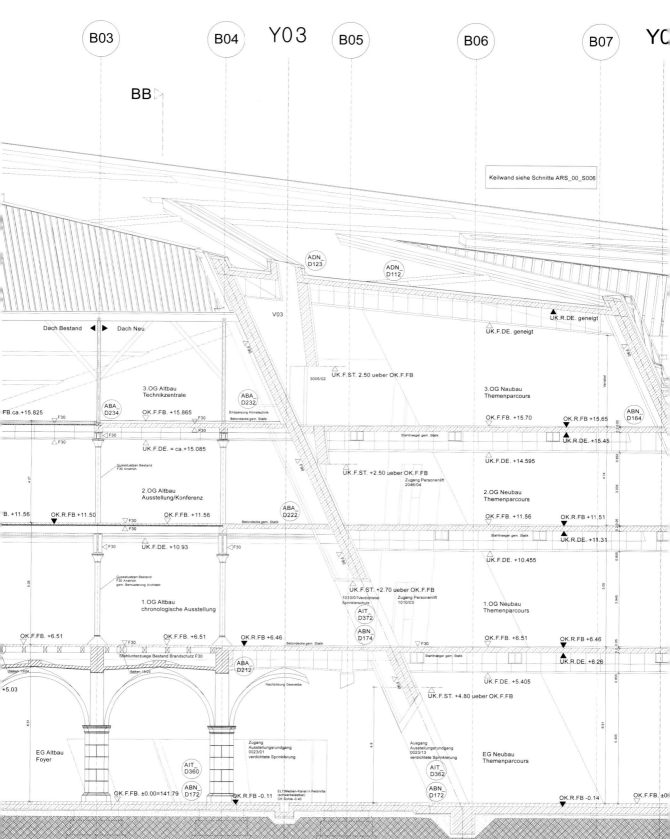

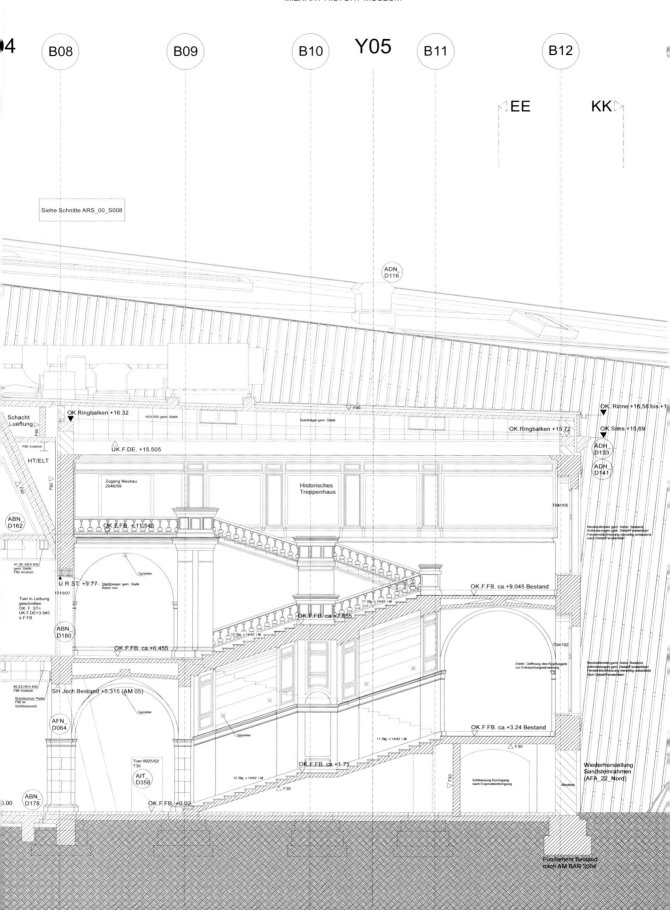

B08   B09   B10   Y05   B11   B12

EE   KK

Siehe Schnitte ARS_00_S008

ADN_
D116

OK. Rinne +16,58 bis +1

Schacht
Lueftung

OK.Ringbalken +16.32   HEA/550 gem. Statik   Stahlträger gem. Statik

OK.Ringbalken +15,72   OK.Sims +15,69

F90 Anstrich

HT/ELT

OK.F.DE. +15.505

ADH_
D133

ADH_
D141

Zugang Neubau
2046/09

Historisches
Treppenhaus

T04/105

Neubaufenster gem. histor. Bestand.
Anforderungen gem. Detail/Fensterliste!
Fensterstockheizung vierseitig umlaufend
nach Detail/Fensterliste

ABN_
D162

OK.F.FB. +11.545

41.36- HEA 400
gem. Statik
F90 Anstrich

Sprinkler

U.R.ST. +9.77   Stahlträger gem. Statik
Beton neu

OK.F.FB. ca.+9.045 Bestand

Tuer in Leibung
geschnitten
OK. F. ST=
UK.F.DE=3.945
ü.F.FB

1010/07

11 Stg. x 14/42 i.M

ABN_
D180

OK.F.FB. ca.+7.855

40.23- HEA 400
F90 Anstrich

OK.F.FB. ca.+6.455

12 Stg. x 14/42 i.M

T04/102

Brandschutz Platte
F90 im
Schlitzbereich

SH Joch Bestand +5.315 (AM 05)

Elektr. Oeffnung des Kippflugels
zur Entrauchungsstroemung

Neubaufenster gem. histor. Bestand,
Anforderungen gem. Detail/Fensterliste!
Fensterstockheizung vierseitig umlaufend
nach Detail/Fensterliste

Sprinkler

AFN_
D064

Sprinkler

OK.F.FB. ca.+3.24 Bestand

11 Stg. x 14/42 i.M

F30

Tuer 0025/02
T30

OK.F.FB. ca.+1.71

Wiederherstellung
Sandsteinrahmen
(AFA_22_Nord)

AIT_
D358

12 Stg. x 14/42 i.M

F30

Schliessung Durchgang
nach Exponateinbringung

F30

Blindfeld

ABN_
D178

OK.F.FB. +0.02

0.00

Fundament Bestand
nach AM BAR 2004

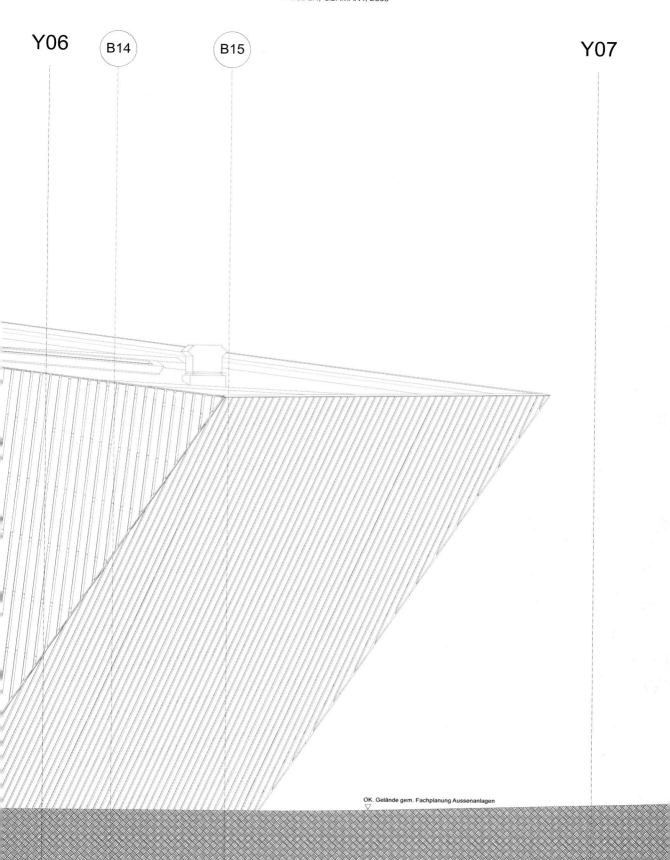

Y06

B14

B15

Y07

OK. Gelände gem. Fachplanung Aussenanlagen

You began your life as a musician and then became an architect.
What is the ongoing role of music in your life and what
are the connections between your musical education and
the architecture that you make?

I DESIGN BUILDINGS AS EXPRESSIVE MUSICAL COMPOSITIONS. THROUGH PRECISE VIBRATIONS I AIM AT EMOTIONAL RESONANCE.

GRAND CANAL SQUARE CREATES A CULTURAL AND COMMERCIAL PRESENCE AT THE HEART OF THE GRAND CANAL HARBOR DEVELOPMENT.

THE PERFORM-ING ARTS CENTER IS INTEGRATED IN AND FLANKED BY EXPRES-SIVE OFFICE BUILDINGS.

FROM THE PLAZA, THE FOYER OF THE THEATER BECOMES A MULTILEVEL STAGE BEHIND THE GLASS CURTAIN OF THE MAIN FACADE.

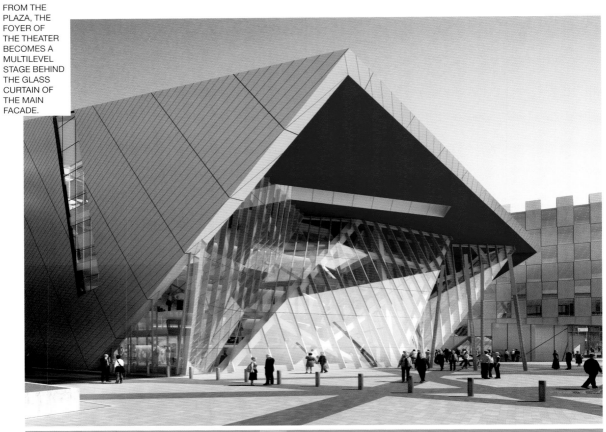

SECTION

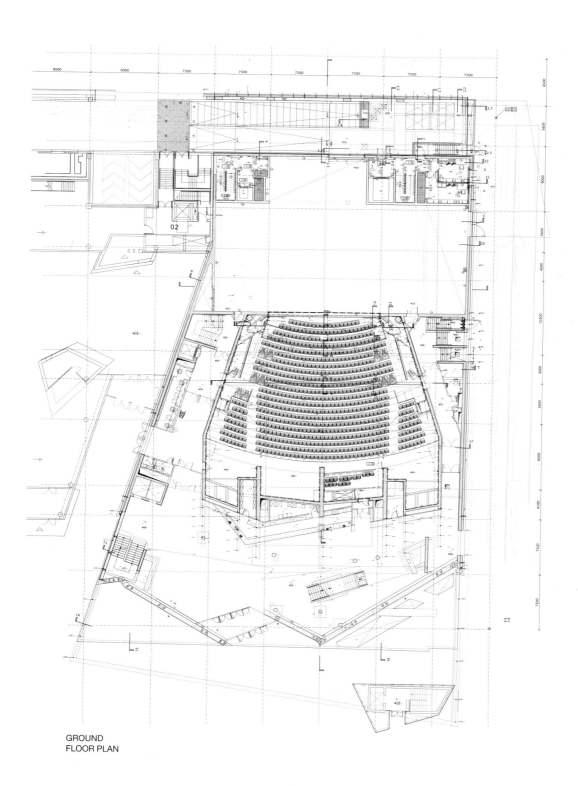

GROUND
FLOOR PLAN

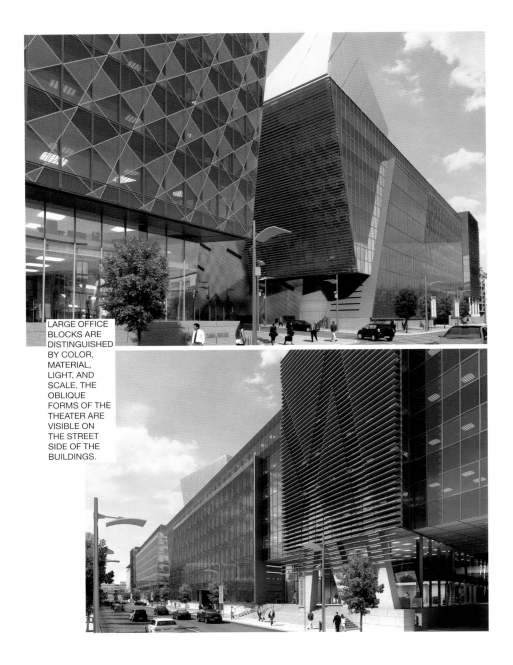

LARGE OFFICE BLOCKS ARE DISTINGUISHED BY COLOR, MATERIAL, LIGHT, AND SCALE. THE OBLIQUE FORMS OF THE THEATER ARE VISIBLE ON THE STREET SIDE OF THE BUILDINGS.

THE INTERIOR OF THE TWO-THOUSAND-SEAT THEATER IS INSPIRED IN PART BY THE HISTORY OF THE GRAND CANAL.

Once one studies your buildings carefully and gets closer
to them, one discovers there is a language that you've created, and within
that language, in fact, there are many variations possible.

THE OPPOR-TUNITY TO ENGAGE IN THAT LANGUAGE IS A HUGE ONE. THE SOCIAL ENGAGEMENT EXPANDS YOUR LANGUAGE.

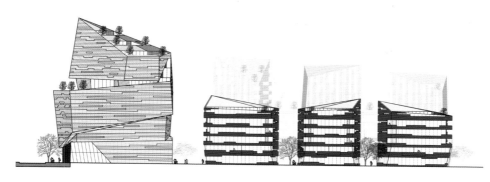

WEST
ELEVATION/
SECTION

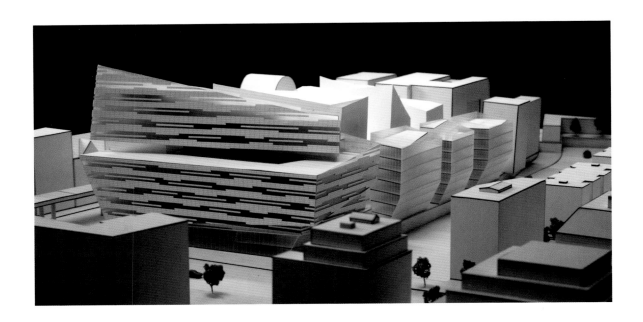

A SPIRALING OFFICE TOWER AND THREE MIXED-USE BLOCKS RISE IN THE HISTORIC CENTER OF HAMBURG. GEOMETRIES SHIFT BETWEEN ROOF AND GROUND LEVEL.

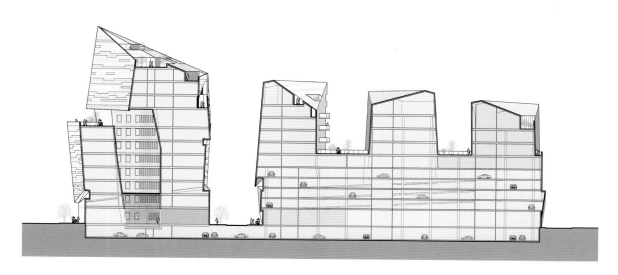

SECTION

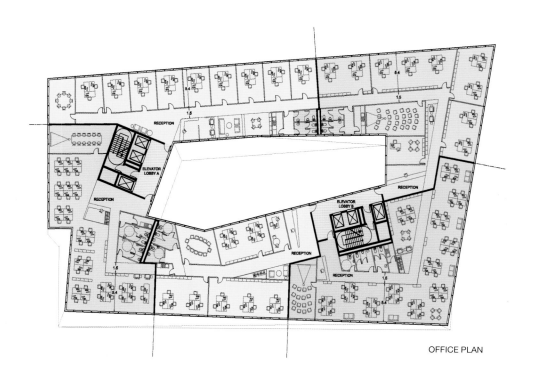

OFFICE PLAN

There is an interesting and perhaps conscious tension
in your media center in Hong Kong between the
Bauhaus modernism of the strip window and the form
of the building, which is just so different.

TOO OFTEN RATIONALITY IS EQUATED WITH FORMULAS. BUT TRUE MODERNITY HAS A POETIC IMPULSE.

THE PLAYFUL
VOLUMES OF
THE BUILD-
ING CONTAIN
HIGH-DENSITY
UNIVERSITY
PROGRAMS.

LIKE A GIANT
CARVED ROCK,
THE CENTER
ECHOES THE
LANDSCAPE.
IT CONTRASTS
WITH NEARBY
LARGE-SCALE
BLOCKS.

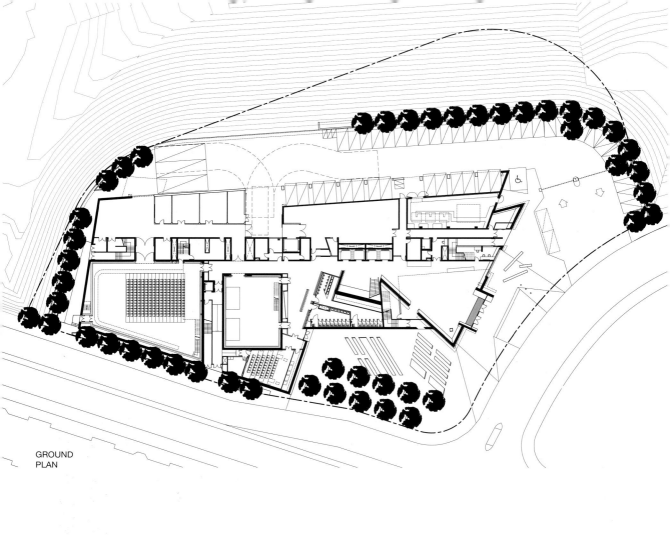

GROUND
PLAN

SECTION

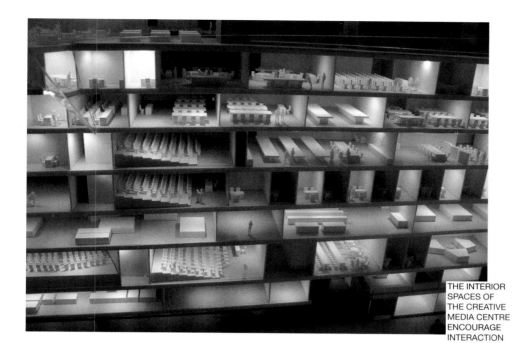

THE INTERIOR SPACES OF THE CREATIVE MEDIA CENTRE ENCOURAGE INTERACTION BETWEEN EVENTS, PRO-GRAMMATIC REQUIRE-MENTS, AND STUDY.

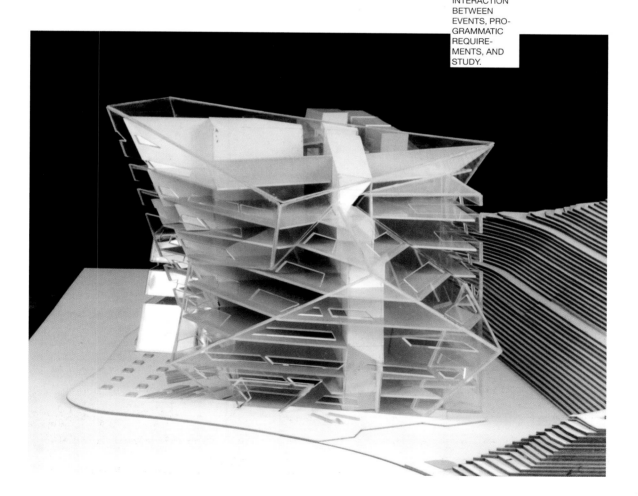

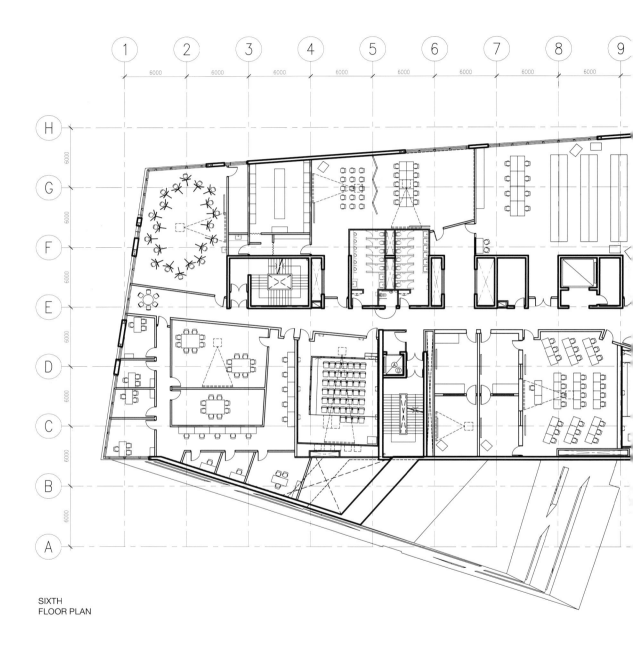

SIXTH
FLOOR PLAN

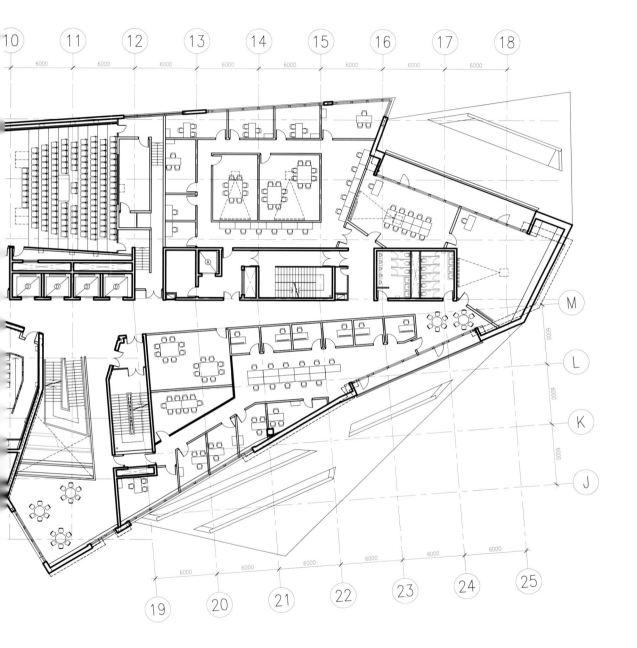

What does it mean to construct a shopping
center within a brand-new city?

IT MEANS RAISING THE EVERYDAYNESS OF SHOPPING INTO AN ICONIC AND MEANINGFUL EXPERIENCE.

THE URBAN
ARCHITEC-
TURE OF THE
SHOPPING
CENTER HAS A
METROPOLITAN
SCALE.

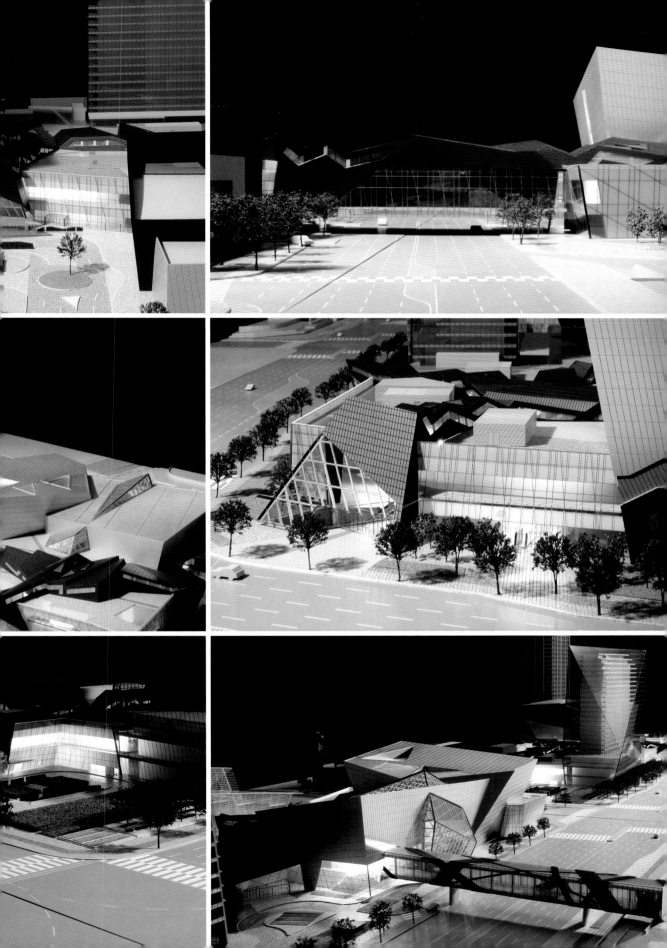

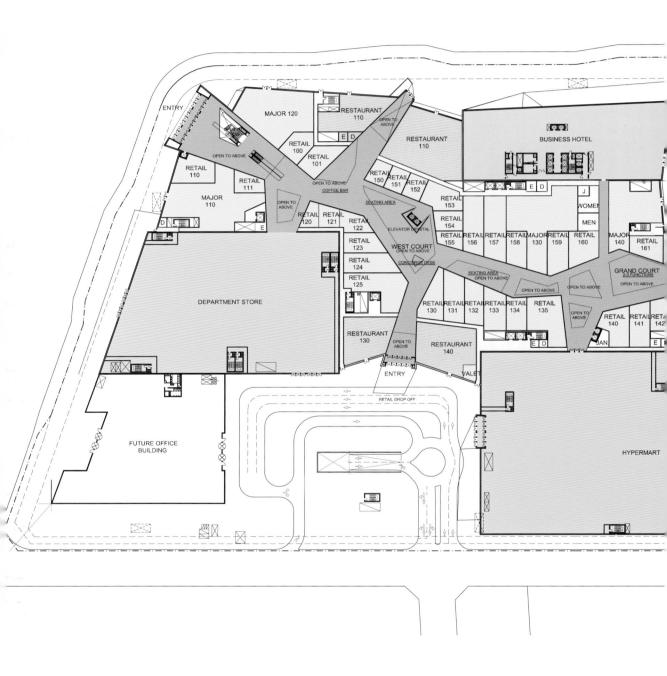

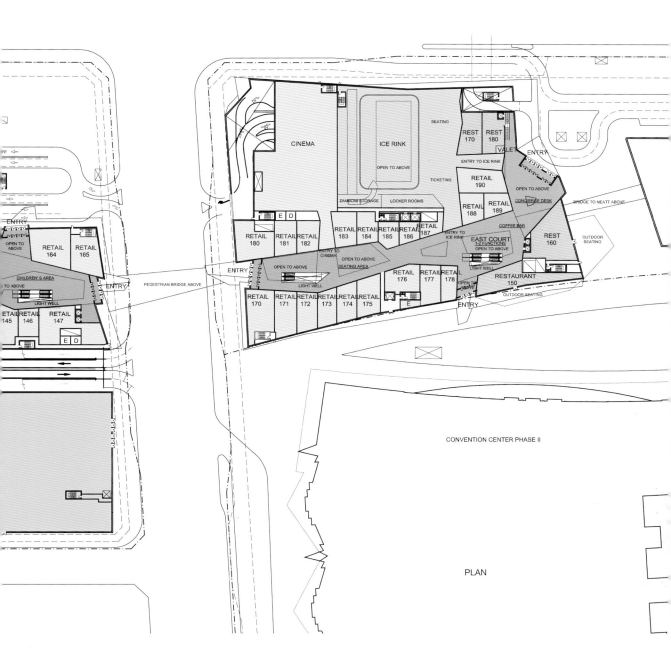

CINEMA

ICE RINK

OPEN TO ABOVE

SEATING

REST 170

REST 180

VALET

ENTRY

ENTRY TO ICE RINK

RETAIL 190

TICKETING

RETAIL 188

RETAIL 189

CONCIERGE DESK

BRIDGE TO NEATT ABOVE

OPEN TO ABOVE

ZAMBONI STORAGE

LOCKER ROOMS

E D

RETAIL 180

RETAIL 181

RETAIL 182

RETAIL 183

RETAIL 184

RETAIL 185

RETAIL 186

RETAIL 187

ENTRY TO ICE RINK

COFFEE BAR

EAST COURT
1-2 FUNCTIONS
OPEN TO ABOVE

REST 160

OUTDOOR SEATING

ENTRY

ENTRY TO CINEMA

OPEN TO ABOVE

SEATING AREA

LIGHT WELL

RETAIL 176

RETAIL 177

RETAIL 178

LIGHT WELL

RESTAURANT 150

RETAIL 164

RETAIL 165

ENTRY

OPEN TO ABOVE

CHILDREN'S AREA
TO ABOVE

LIGHT WELL

ENTRY

PEDESTRIAN BRIDGE ABOVE

RETAIL 170

RETAIL 171

RETAIL 172

RETAIL 173

RETAIL 174

RETAIL 175

E

OPEN TO ABOVE

OUTDOOR SEATING

ENTRY

RETAIL 145

RETAIL 146

RETAIL 147

E D

CONVENTION CENTER PHASE II

PLAN

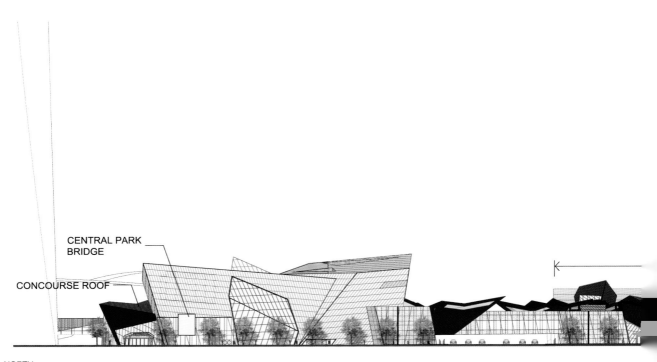

CENTRAL PARK
BRIDGE

CONCOURSE ROOF

NORTH
ELEVATION

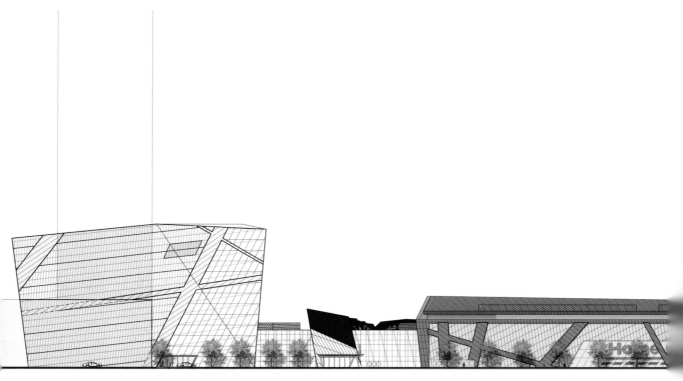

SOUTH
ELEVATION

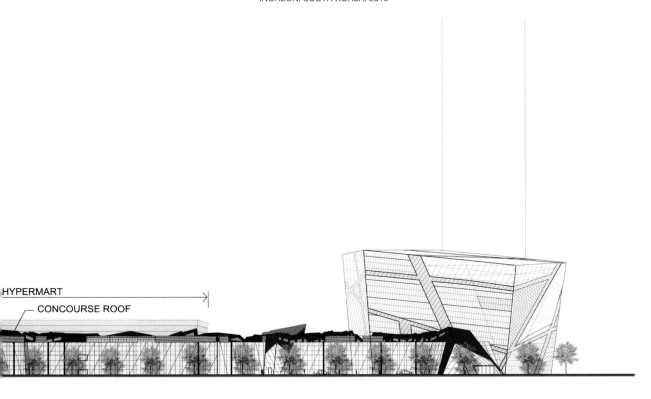

HYPERMART

CONCOURSE ROOF

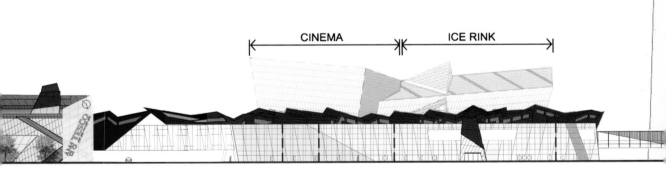

CINEMA

ICE RINK

Are developers a stumbling block to good design?

THE MARKET-PLACE IS OFTEN ASSOCIATED WITH CYNICISM AND EXPLOITATION. BUT IN MY EXPE-RIENCE, THAT IS NOT AT ALL THE REAL OR THE WHOLE PICTURE.

URBAN
DESIGN AND
ARCHITECTURE
INCREASE THE
DENSITY OF A
CENTRAL SITE
IN JERUSALEM
AND LINK IT
TO THE OLD
CITY AND
SURROUNDING
NEIGHBOR-
HOODS.

INNER COURT-
YARDS AND
SURPRISING
STREETS
EXTEND THE
HISTORIC
STRUCTURE
OF THE
MUNICIPALITY.

THE SITING OF
THE INDIVIDUAL
COMPONENTS
RESPONDS
TO THE GATE-
WAYS AND HIS-
TORIC VISTAS
OF THE CITY.

GROUND
PLAN, RETAIL

EIGHTH
FLOOR PLAN

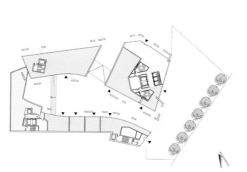

GROUND
PLAN, TOWER

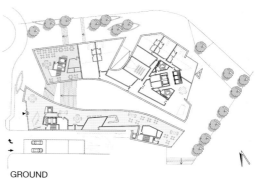

GROUND
PLAN

Your skyscrapers have very distinctive forms,
and they do things that engineers could not have done if you
had been doing them fifteen or twenty years ago.

CERTAINLY THERE ARE NEW POSSIBILITIES, BUT I DON'T DESIGN JUST FOR THE SAKE OF EXPERIMENTAL FORMS.

A SUITE OF UNDULATING TOWERS CHARACTERIZES THE RESIDENTIAL DEVELOPMENT AT THE ENTRANCE TO KEPPEL HARBOR. THE SLEEK CURVING FORMS OF DIFFERING HEIGHTS CREATE GRACEFUL OPENINGS AND GAPS.

THE ROOFTOP
GARDENS
ALLOW FOR
UNOBSTRUCTED
VIEWS OF
THE BAY AND
THE HORIZON
BEYOND.

SITE PLAN

A DUET OF DOUBLE-CURVED TOWERS AND URBAN VILLAS CONSTITUTES THIS NEW WATERFRONT DEVELOPMENT.

MAX. BUILDABLE HEIGT - 178 AMSL
TALL TOWER

MAX. BUILDABLE HEIGT - 120 AMSL
SMALL TOWER

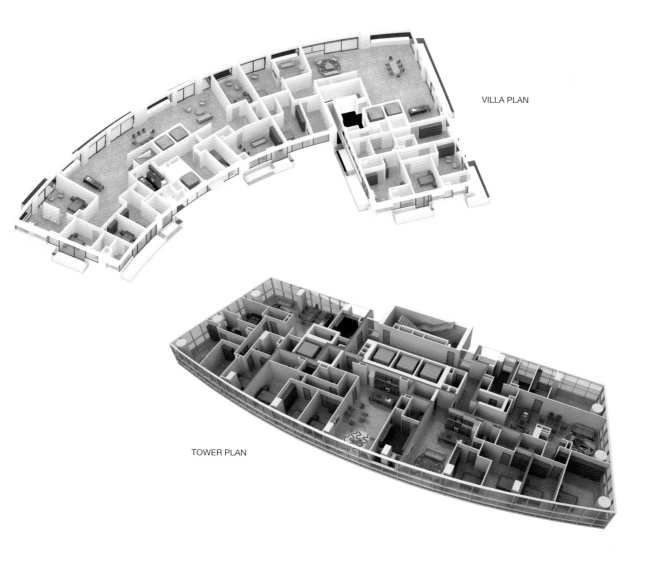

VILLA PLAN

TOWER PLAN

What is the experience of trying to do what we might call serious
architecture in Las Vegas, and how did you approach that?
How different is it from other projects given that
you're not designing distinctive forms that may play
against an otherwise dull cityscape?

ROBERT VENTURI SPOKE ELOQUENTLY OF "LEARNING FROM LAS VEGAS," BUT NOW THE CITY NEEDS MORE THAN SIGNAGE.

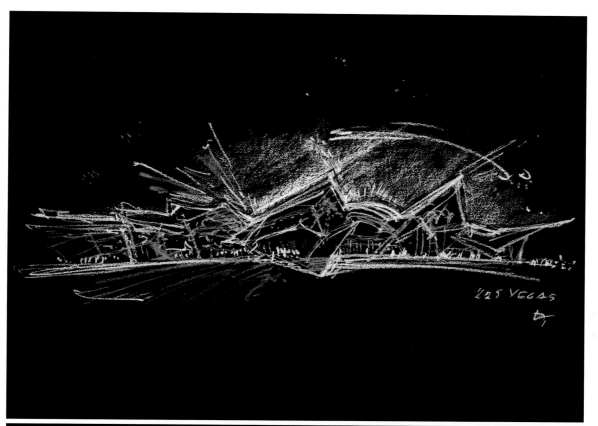

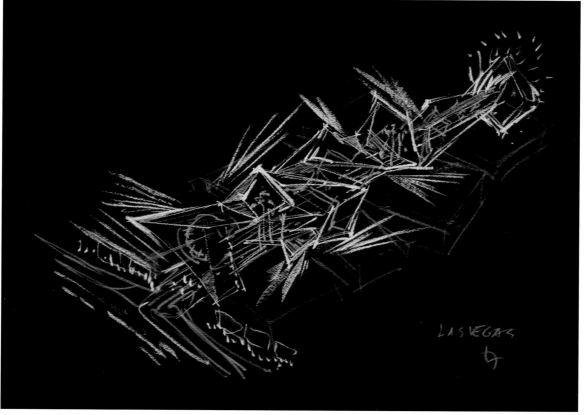

SHARDS OF
GLASS FORM
THE BASE FOR
RESIDENTIAL
TOWERS,
HOTELS, AND
CASINOS.

COLLISIONS, SUPERIMPOSI- TIONS, AND INTERSEC- TIONS ARE THE EBB AND FLOW IN AN EVER-MOVING SPACE.

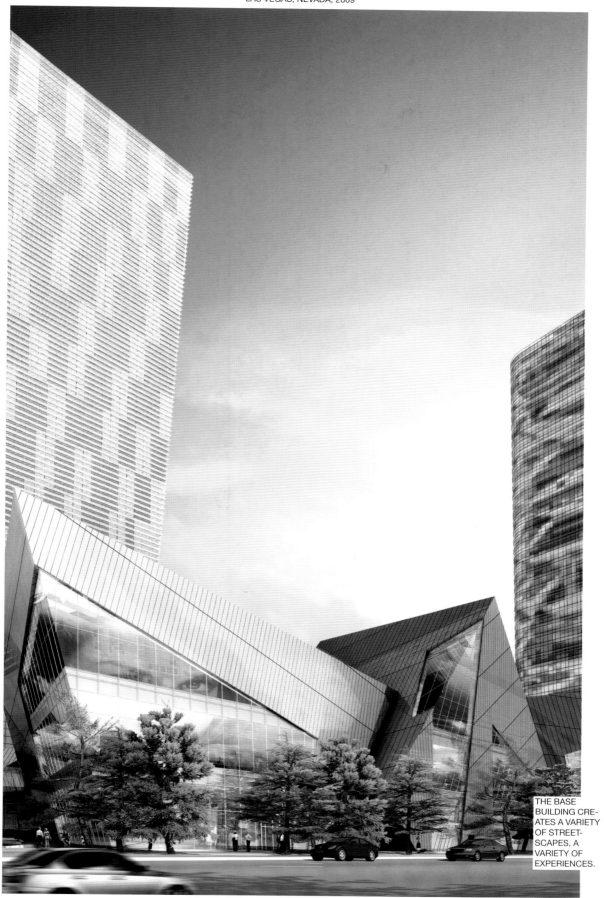

THE BASE
BUILDING CRE-
ATES A VARIETY
OF STREET-
SCAPES, A
VARIETY OF
EXPERIENCES.

MGM MIRAGE
CITYCENTER
CREATES
SOPHISTI-
CATED ADVEN-
TURES FOR
THE PUBLIC.

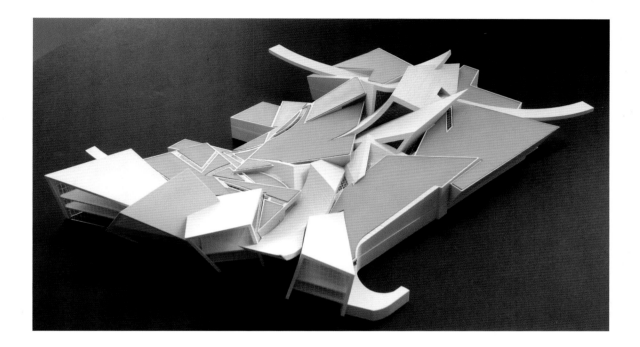

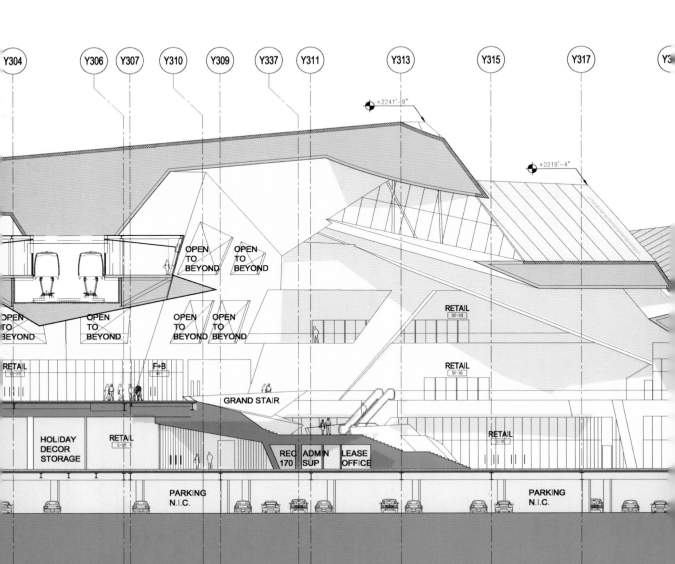

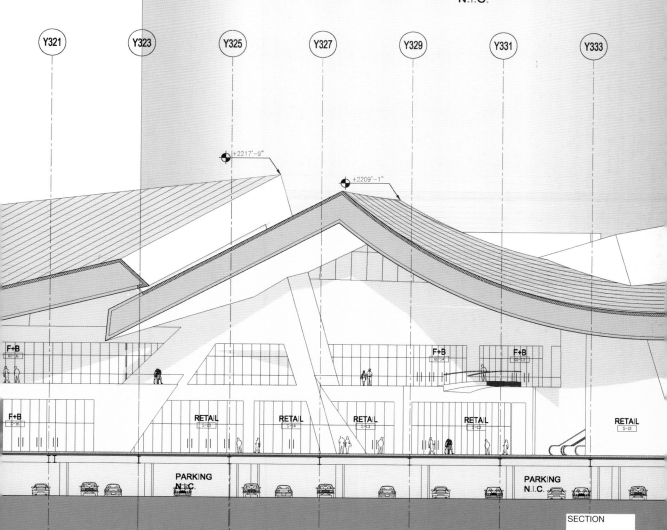

LIFESTYLE HOTEL
N.I.C.

Y321 Y323 Y325 Y327 Y329 Y331 Y333

+2217'-9"

+2209'-1"

F+B
B1-16

F+B
GF-14

F+B
B1-13

F+B
S-16

RETAIL
S-15

RETAIL
S-14

RETAIL
S-13

RETAIL
S-13

RETAIL
S-10

PARKING
N.I.C.

PARKING
N.I.C.

SECTION

The thing that always strikes me about your work is that it is
responsive to context without being imitative of context.
It's often physically very, very different, but it is not wholly self-
referential. It is full of references to other things.

THE CONTEXT IS NEVER INERT. YOU JUST HAVE TO TAP INTO IT TO REVEAL ITS POTENTIAL. EVEN A TINY BUILDING CAN CHANGE A NEIGHBORHOOD.

FOUR BUILD-
INGS MERGE
ON HOLLOWAY
ROAD.

THE ENTRANCE
PLAZA
BECKONS
WITH LARGE
WINDOWS.

PASSERSBY ON
THE STREET
ARE OFFERED
GLIMPSES INTO
THE SEMINAR
ROOMS.

THE BUILDING CONSISTS OF THREE INTERSECTING ELEMENTS; THE EXISTING BUILDING IS THE FOURTH. ONE CREATES A CONNECTION BETWEEN THE PUBLIC, THE GRADUATE CENTRE, AND THE UNIVERSITY; THE SECOND GESTURES TOWARD THE TUBE CONNECTION; AND THE THIRD STITCHES THE BUILDING INTO THE CONTEXT OF HOLLOWAY ROAD.

SIMPLE AND
BOLD INTERIOR
SPACES
ACCOMMODATE
A VARIETY OF
EVENTS. THE
GEOMETRIC
OPENINGS
FRAME SIGNIFI-
CANT VISTAS.

THE CENTER
SERVES BOTH
GRADUATE
STUDENTS AND
THE LARGER
COMMUNITY.

A job that didn't happen was your extension to the V&A. You must regret that at this point, even though many other things, wonderful things, have happened since.

ARCHITECTURE DOESN'T DEPEND ON COMMISSIONS ONLY. A MEANINGFUL PROJECT IS NEVER LOST BECAUSE IT IS PART OF AN ONGOING QUEST.

THE EXTEN-
SION TO THE
V&A MAINTAINS
A DIALOGUE
WITH THE
SURROUNDING
EAVES AND
RIDGE LINES.

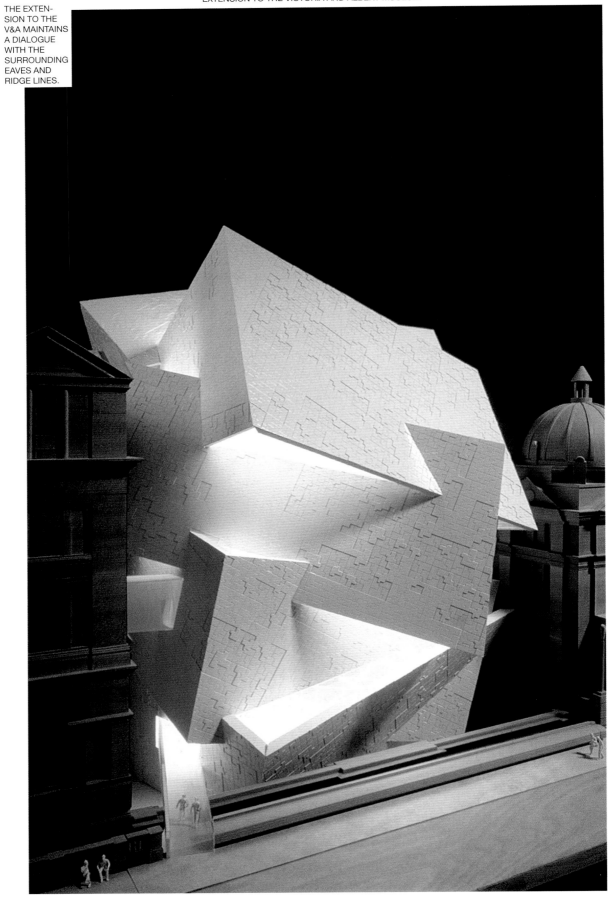

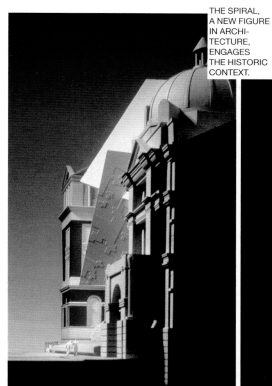

THE SPIRAL,
A NEW FIGURE
IN ARCHI-
TECTURE,
ENGAGES
THE HISTORIC
CONTEXT.

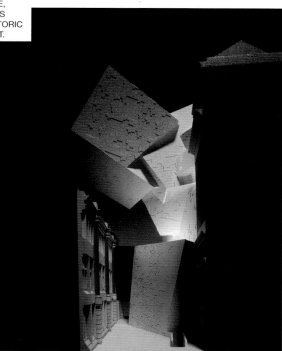

INTERNAL AND
EXTERNAL
SPACES ENER-
GIZE A NEW
ENTRANCE ON
EXHIBITION
ROAD.

THE EXTEN-
SION OPENS A
PLURALITY OF
DIRECTIONS
ALONG MANY
DIFFERENT
TRAJECTORIES,
PROVIDING
MULTIPLE
ROUTES,
SPACES, AND
AMBIENCES
FOR VISITORS.
THE BUILDING
USES A SIMPLE,
CONTINUOUS,
INTERLOCKING
WALL SYSTEM
TO CREATE AND
ARTICULATE
FUNCTIONS.

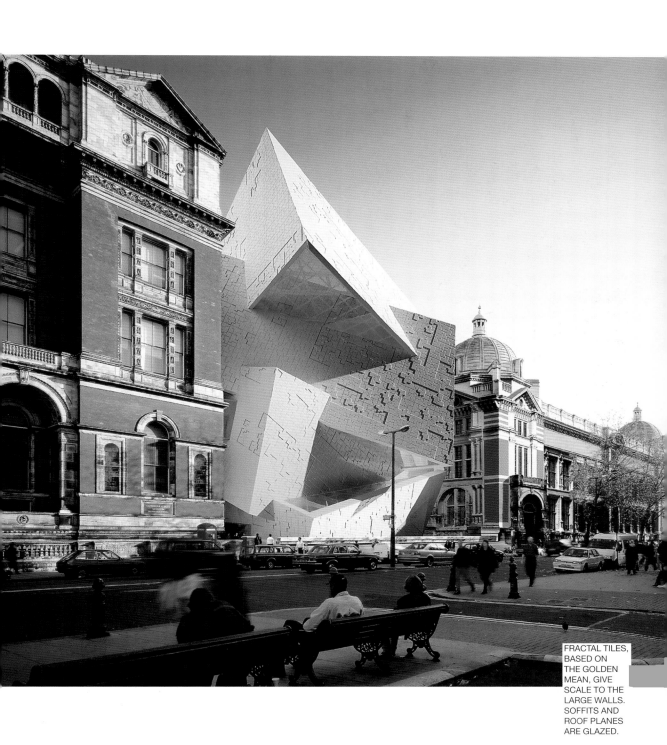

FRACTAL TILES,
BASED ON
THE GOLDEN
MEAN, GIVE
SCALE TO THE
LARGE WALLS.
SOFFITS AND
ROOF PLANES
ARE GLAZED.

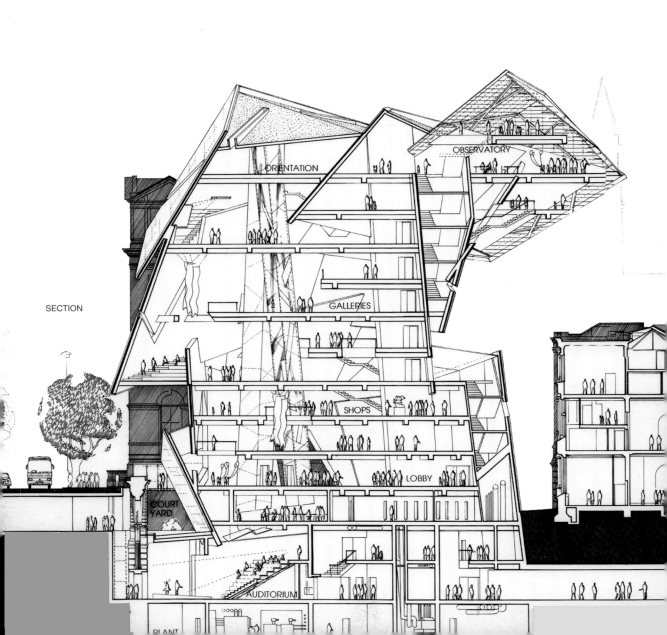

SECTION

ORIENTATION

OBSERVATORY

GALLERIES

SHOPS

LOBBY

COURT YARD

AUDITORIUM

PLANT

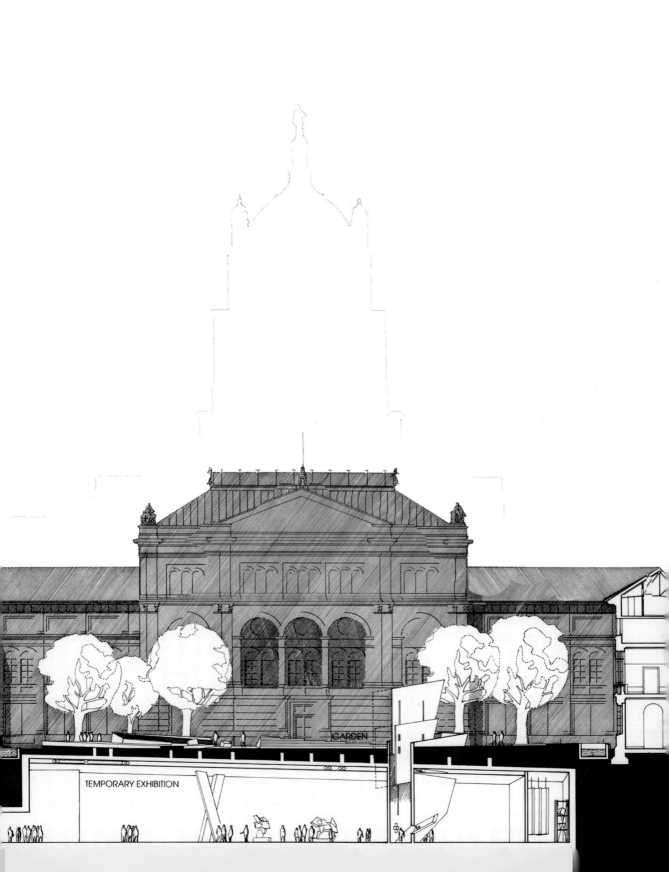

GARDEN

TEMPORARY EXHIBITION

For all the distinctions between your buildings, say between the Jewish Museum, the Denver Art Museum, the Contemporary Jewish Museum, and the Royal Ontario Museum, one could also certainly see a familial relationship.

THE TRUE SIGNATURE OF A BUILDING IS NOT A FASHION OR A STYLE BUT A CHARACTER THAT RESISTS APPROPRIATION. ◆

THE AIR
SHARD, ONE
OF THREE
INTERLOCK-
ING SHARDS
THAT MAKE UP
THE MUSEUM,
GIVES A PAN-
ORAMIC VIEW
OF THE CITY.

THE AIR
SHARD,
HALF OPEN
TO THE SKY,
INTERSECTS
THE EARTH
SHARD.

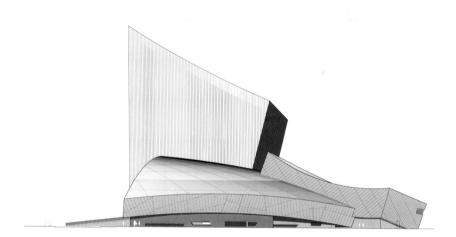

WEST
ELEVATION

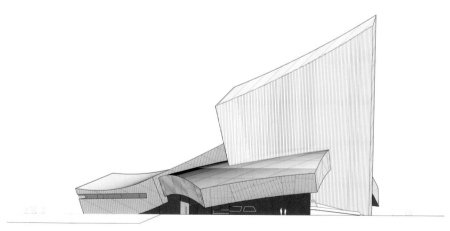

EAST
ELEVATION

THE WATER,
EARTH, AND
AIR SHARDS
REPRESENT
THE THREE
ARENAS OF
WAR.

THE MAIN ENTRANCE TO THE BUILDING IS THROUGH THE AIR SHARD. THE EDUCATION WING IS UNDER THE EARTH SHARD.

THE AIR
SHARD, OPEN
TO THE
WEATHER,
CUTS THROUGH
THE STRUC-
TURE OF THE
MUSEUM. AT
THE TOP IS
A WALKWAY
TO THE
OBSERVATORY.

SOUND AND
LIGHT SHOWS
DISSOLVE THE
EXHIBITION
SPACES.

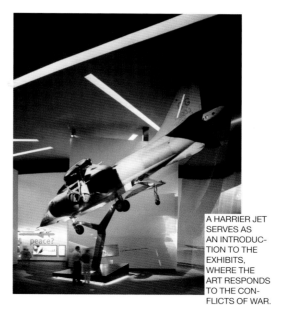

A HARRIER JET
SERVES AS
AN INTRODUC-
TION TO THE
EXHIBITS,
WHERE THE
ART RESPONDS
TO THE CON-
FLICTS OF WAR.

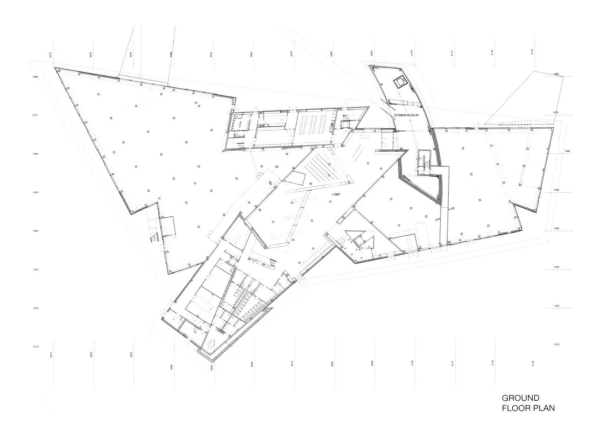

GROUND
FLOOR PLAN

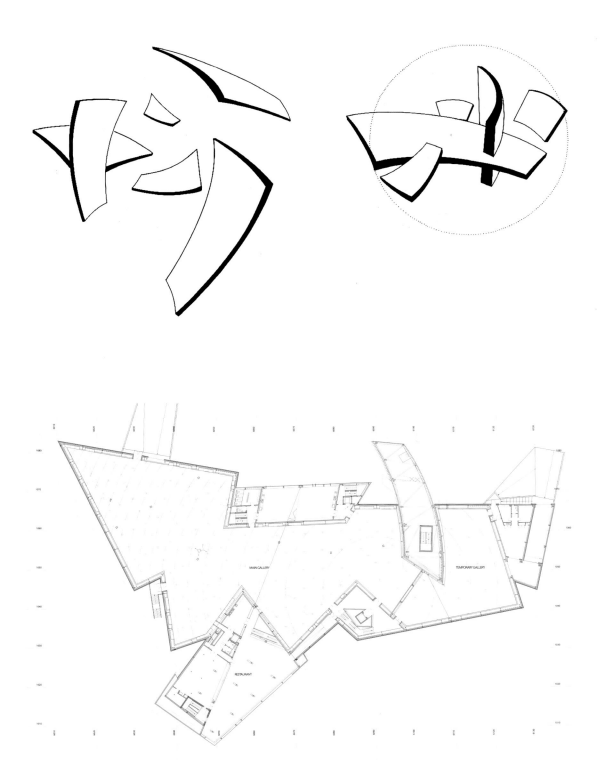

MAIN GALLERY
FLOOR PLAN

It seems to me as if you see enlivening the cultural life of a
city as part of the program of all of your buildings.

I DON'T MAKE A DISTINCTION BETWEEN URBAN PLANNING AND ARCHITECTURE. I SEE THEM AS INSEPARABLE PROTAGONISTS IN THE MEMORY OF THE CITY.

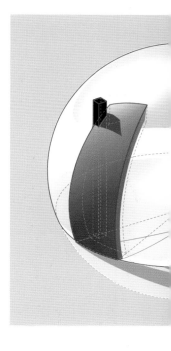

THE SKY-
SCRAPER AND
THE TWO
NEIGHBORING
TOWERS FORM
A CENTRAL
PLAZA IN THE
PARK.

THE FORM OF
THE CONTEM-
PORARY ART
MUSEUM WAS
INSPIRED BY
LEONARDO DA
VINCI. A PER-
FECT SQUARE
AT THE LOBBY
LEVEL, IT IS
TRANSFORMED
INTO A CIRCLE
AT THE TOP.

THE CURVA-
TURE AND
UNIQUE
PROFILE OF
THE TOWER
RELATE
SPECIFICALLY
TO SUN AND
SHADE. THE
BUILDING HAS
A STRONG
CENTRAL
CORE, TWO
LATERAL BRAC-
ING TRUSSES,
AND A STAN-
DARD FLOOR
PLATE.

LOGGIAS AND
BALCONIES
FIGURE IN
THE HOUSING
BLOCKS.

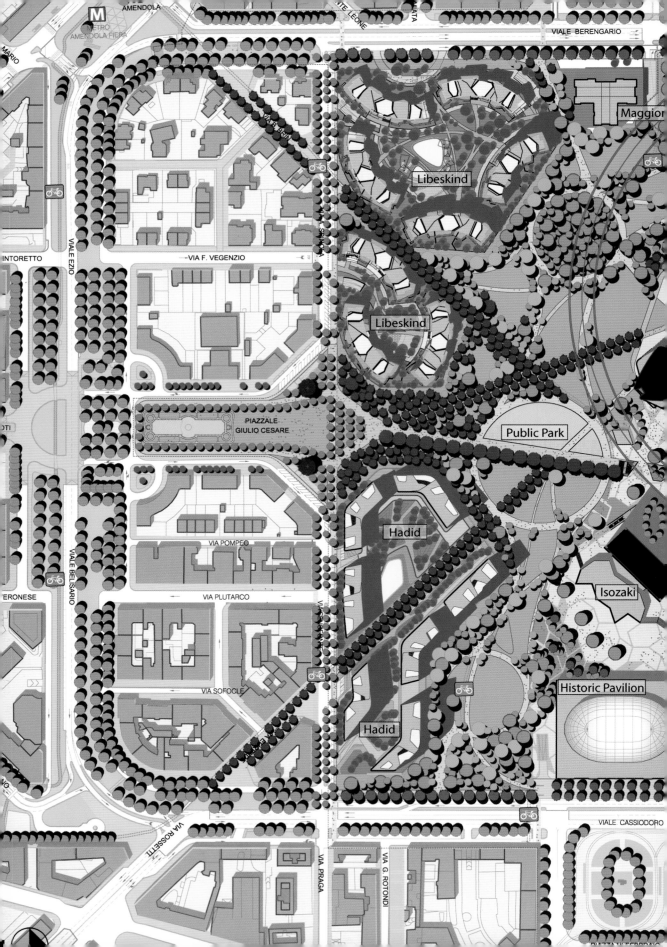

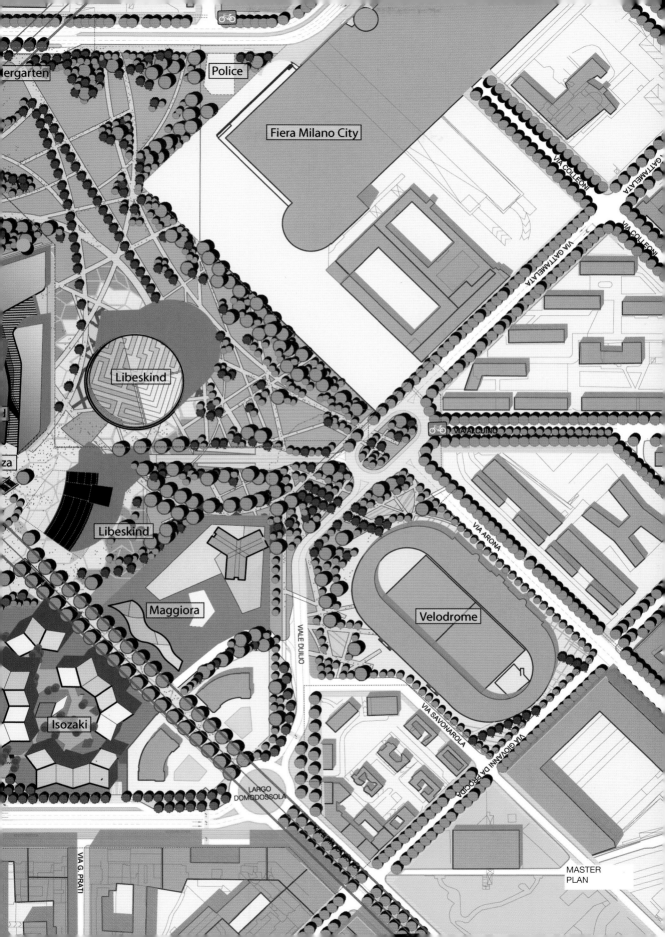

Tiergarten

Police

Fiera Milano City

VIA COLLEONI

VIA GATTAMELATA

VIA COLLEONI

Libeskind

VIA ALCUINO

Libeskind

VIA ARONA

Maggiora

Velodrome

Isozaki

VIALE DUILIO

VIA SAVONAROLA

VIA GIOVANNI DA PROCIDA

LARGO
DOMODOSSOLA

VIA G. PRATI

MASTER
PLAN

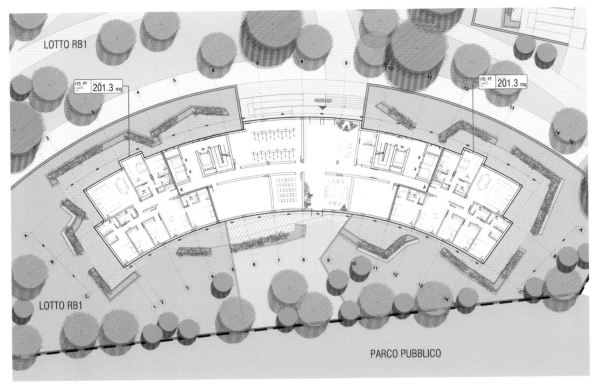

LOTTO RB1

201.3 mq

201.3 mq

LOTTO RB1

PARCO PUBBLICO

GROUND
PLAN

SITE PLAN

VIEWS, ORIENTATION, SUSTAINABILITY, AND ATTENTION TO LIFESTYLE CHARACTERIZE THE HOUSING. LOCATED ON THE PERIPHERY, IT MAXIMIZES PARK SPACE.

THREE HIGH-
RISES FLANK A
HUGE CENTRAL
PARK. THE
MUSEUM AND
COMMERCIAL
SPACE EXTEND
THE PLAZA.

You are known for so many large-scale projects.
What about the other end of the architectural
spectrum—private homes?

I AM DESIGNING A HOUSE AS AN ART EXPERIENCE. IT'S THINKING OUTSIDE THE GLASS BOX.

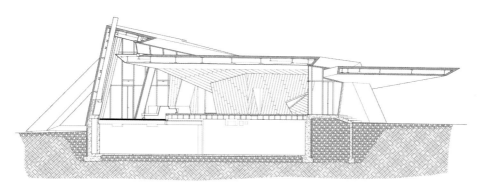

SECTION

THE OBJECTS
THAT MAKE
UP THE BUILD-
ING REVEAL
THEMSELVES
GRADUALLY.

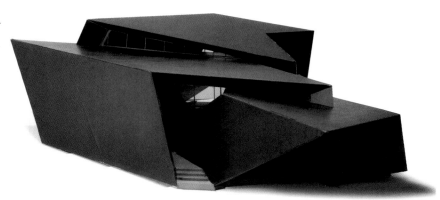

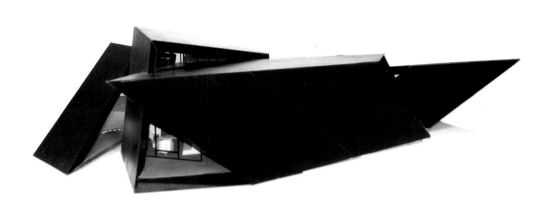

THE CHOREOG-
RAPHY OF THE
WALLS SHAPES
THE DANCE OF
THE VOLUMES.
LIGHT INFUSES
THE INTERIOR.

18.36.54

TERRACE

K

LIVING

DINING

TERRACE

DN

PLAN

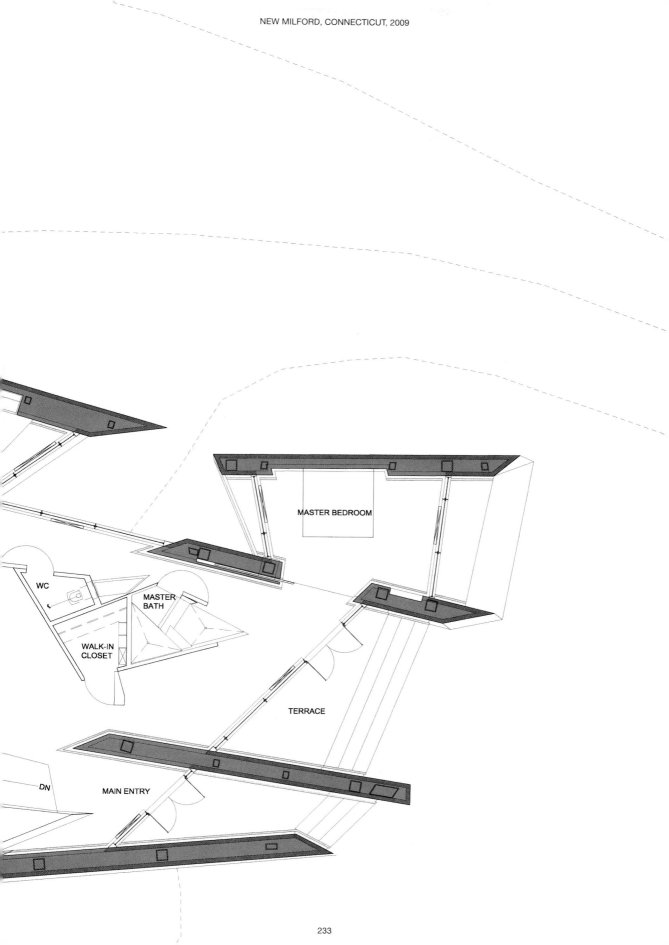

MASTER BEDROOM

WC

MASTER
BATH

WALK-IN
CLOSET

TERRACE

DN

MAIN ENTRY

Let's talk for a moment about the very large project that brought
you back to New York, which was the Ground Zero
master plan, which ironically put you—even more than the
Jewish Museum—into international attention.

I SHAPED GROUND ZERO WITH A MASTER PLAN THAT IS BASED ON MEMORY AND IMBUED WITH THE SPIRIT OF LIBERTY.

THE GREAT SLURRY WALL, DESIGNED TO HOLD BACK THE HUDSON RIVER, IS THE MOST DRAMATIC ELEMENT TO HAVE SURVIVED THE ATTACKS OF SEPTEMBER 11, 2001. THE EXPOSED WALL OFFERS A PLACE TO CONTEMPLATE THE VASTNESS OF THE TRAGEDY.

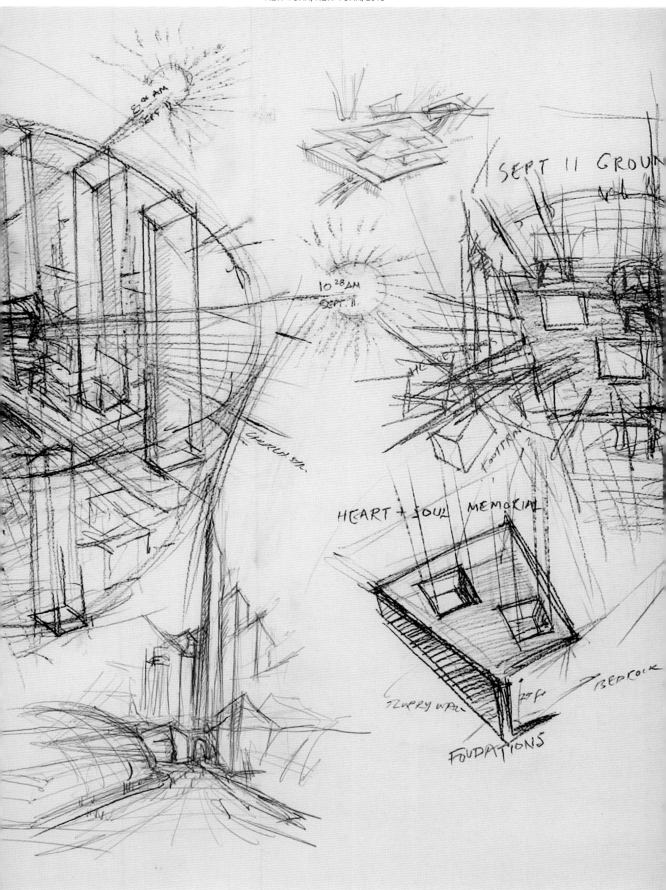

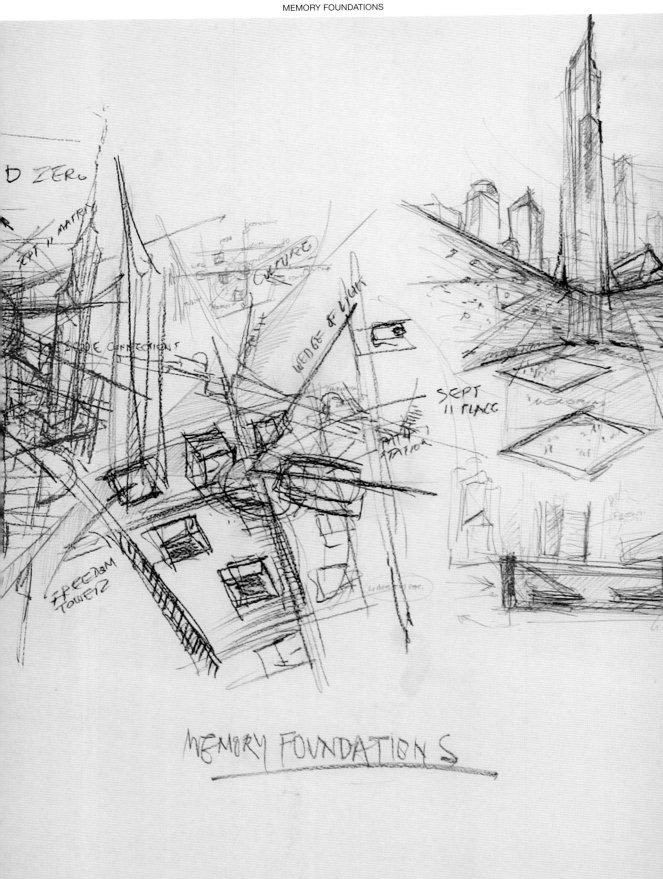

MEMORY FOUNDATIONS

① THE HEART AND THE SOUL:
MEMORY FOUNDATIONS

MEMORIAL SITE EXPOSES
GROUND ZERO
ALL THE WAY DOWN TO THE
BEDROCK FOUNDATIONS.

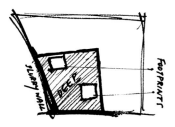

REVEALING THE HEROIC FOUNDATIONS
OF DEMOCRACY FOR ALL TO SEE.

② SEPTEMBER 11 MATRIX

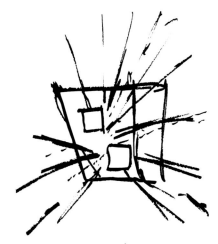

HEROES LINES
TO GROUND ZERO

③ WEDGE OF LIGHT / PARK OF HEROES

SUNLIGHT ON SEPTEMBER 11
MARKING THE PRECISE
TIME OF THE EVENT.

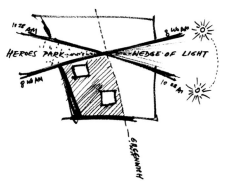

④ CULTURE AT HEART:
PROTECTIVE FILTER AND OPEN
ACCESS TO HALLOWED GROUND

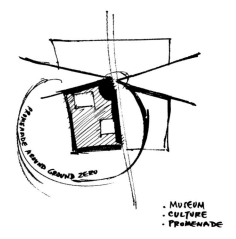

. MUSEUM
. CULTURE
. PROMENADE

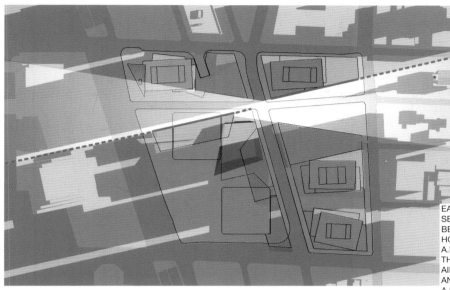

EACH YEAR ON SEPTEMBER 11, BETWEEN THE HOURS OF 8:46 A.M., WHEN THE FIRST AIRPLANE HIT, AND 10:28 A.M., WHEN THE SECOND TOWER COL-LAPSED, THE SUN SHINES WITHOUT SHADOW, A PERPETUAL TRIBUTE TO ALTRUISM AND COURAGE.

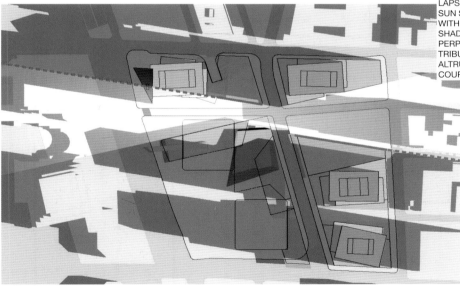

THE COMPETI-
TION PRO-
POSAL SHOWS
A CENTRAL
MEMORIAL
AND A RING OF
SKYSCRAPERS
CULMINAT-
ING IN THE
FREEDOM
TOWER.

THE MASS-
ING OF THE
COMPETITION
PROPOSAL
INITIATES THE
SPIRAL OF
TOWERS IN
THE CURRENT
DESIGN.

THE MEMORIAL SITE, WHICH INCLUDES THE FOOTPRINTS OF THE TOWERS AND A VISITOR ORIENTATION CENTER, REMAINS PROTECTED FROM THE ACTIVITIES OF A REVITALIZED NEIGHBORHOOD.

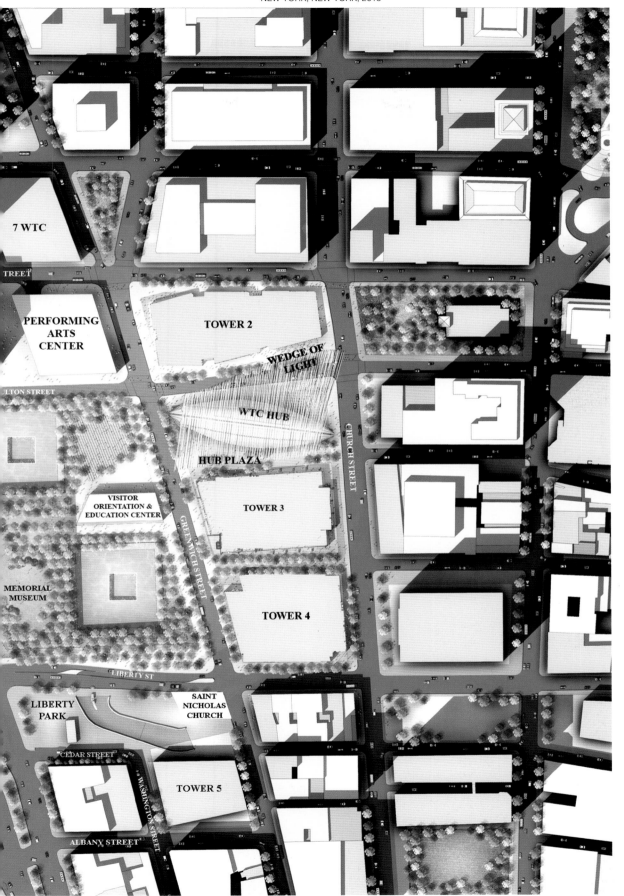

7 WTC

TREET

PERFORMING
ARTS
CENTER

TOWER 2

WEDGE OF
LIGHT

WTC HUB

ULTON STREET

HUB PLAZA

CHURCH STREET

VISITOR
ORIENTATION &
EDUCATION CENTER

TOWER 3

GREENWICH STREET

MEMORIAL
MUSEUM

TOWER 4

LIBERTY ST

LIBERTY
PARK

SAINT
NICHOLAS
CHURCH

CEDAR STREET

WASHINGTON STREET

TOWER 5

ALBANY STREET

GARDENS OF
THE WORLD,
AS THE 1776-
FOOT-TALL
SPIRE WAS
NAMED IN THE
COMPETITION
PROPOSAL,
EVIDENCES
VITALITY IN
THE FACE
OF DANGER
AND OPTIMISM
IN THE AFTER-
MATH OF
TRAGEDY.

THE WEDGE OF
LIGHT PLAZA
OF THE ORIGI-
NAL PROPOSAL
CREATES A
NEW URBAN
SPACE.

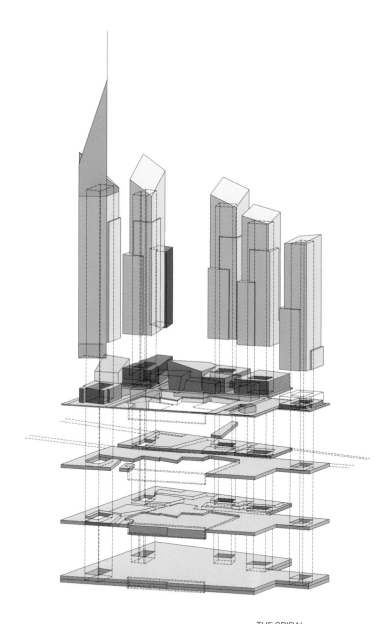

THE SPIRAL
OF TOWERS
AROUND THE
MEMORIAL IS
SUPPORTED
BY A COMPLEX,
SEVENTY-
FIVE-FOOT
UNDERSTORY.

THE SLURRY WALL DELINEATES THE MEMORIAL SITE.

THE WEDGE OF LIGHT PLAZA IN THE COMPETITION PROPOSAL IS CREATED BY THE CENTRAL AXIS OF THE PATH TERMINAL AND THE SOUTHERN FACE OF TOWER TWO. IN THE CENTER IS THE PROPOSED MUSEUM.

You've designed an unusual tower for New York.
What was the idea behind it?

I WANTED TO DESIGN A BUILDING THAT REDEFINES THE TOWER NOT THROUGH SURFACE BUT THROUGH FUNCTION.

PROPOSED

THE BUILDING
IS OFFSET
FROM ITS
NEIGHBORS
TO MAXIMIZE
LIGHT AND
AIR WHILE
SAFEGUARD-
ING VIEWS.
THE TOWER
IS ALSO SET
BACK FROM
THE STREETS
TO ALLOW
SUNLIGHT TO
REACH STREET
LEVEL.

LARGE SPIRAL-
ING GARDENS,
WHICH
CONTINUE
THE GREEN
OF MADISON
SQUARE PARK,
BREAK UP THE
BODY OF THE
TOWER.

THE NEW STRUCTURE IS BUILT UPON AN EXISTING BUILDING ON A HISTORICALLY DYNAMIC SITE.

THE TOWER
PRESERVES
THE FACADE
OF THE BASE
BUILDING
AND ITS
RELATIONSHIP
TO ITS SUR-
ROUNDINGS.

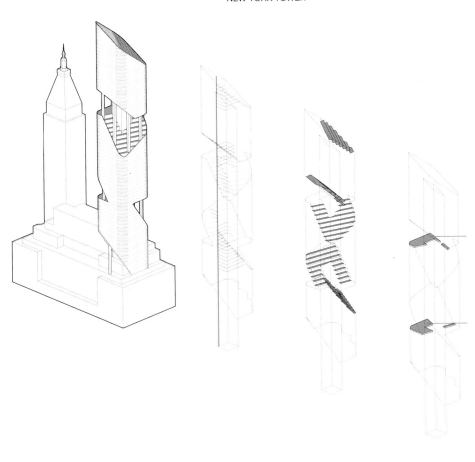

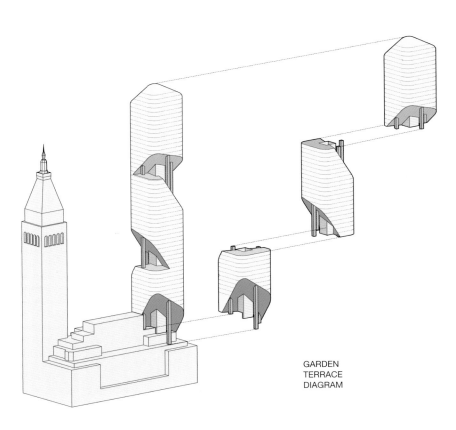

GARDEN
TERRACE
DIAGRAM

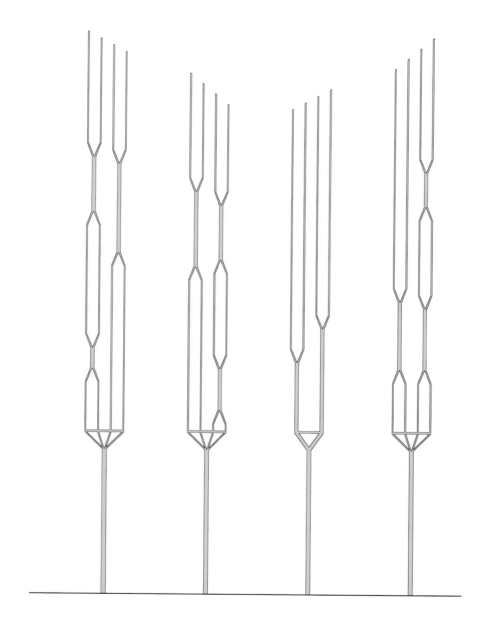

STRUCTURAL
ELEVATION

48th- 54th FLOOR RESIDENTIAL
+ 871'-4 $\frac{1}{2}$"- 936'-10 $\frac{1}{2}$"
7,118 SF

35th- 40th FLOOR RESIDENTIAL
+ 729'-5 $\frac{1}{2}$"- 784'-0 $\frac{1}{2}$"
2,322 SF

34th FLOOR AMENITY LEVEL
+ 718'- 6 $\frac{1}{2}$"
3,189 SF

25th - 33rd FLOOR RESIDENTIAL
+ 620'- 3 $\frac{1}{2}$"- 707'-7 $\frac{1}{2}$"
4,852 SF

11th - 19th FLOOR RESIDENTIAL
+ 467'- 5 $\frac{1}{2}$"- 554'-9 $\frac{1}{2}$"
3,325 SF

10th FLOOR AMENITY LEVEL
+ 456'-6 $\frac{1}{2}$"
3,428 SF

2nd - 9th FLOOR RESIDENTIAL
+ 369'-2 $\frac{3}{4}$"- 445'-7 $\frac{1}{2}$"
4,286 SF

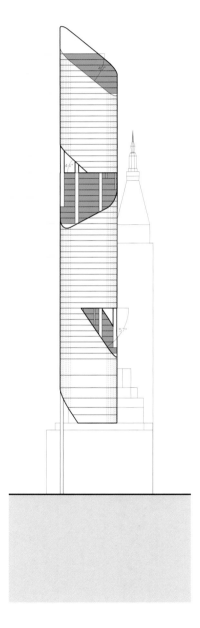

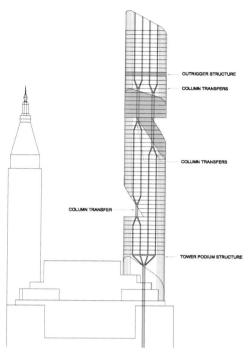

OUTRIGGER STRUCTURE
COLUMN TRANSFERS

COLUMN TRANSFERS

COLUMN TRANSFER

TOWER PODIUM STRUCTURE

**SOUTH
ELEVATION**

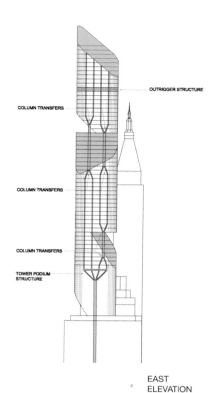

OUTRIGGER STRUCTURE

COLUMN TRANSFERS

COLUMN TRANSFERS

COLUMN TRANSFERS

TOWER PODIUM
STRUCTURE

**EAST
ELEVATION**

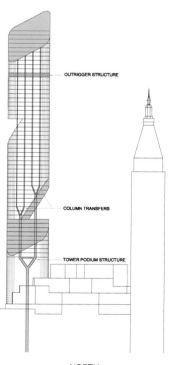

OUTRIGGER STRUCTURE

COLUMN TRANSFERS

TOWER PODIUM STRUCTURE

**NORTH
ELEVATION**

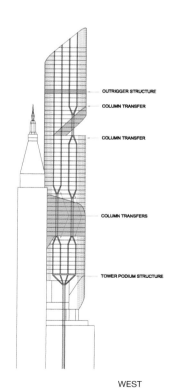

OUTRIGGER STRUCTURE
COLUMN TRANSFER

COLUMN TRANSFER

COLUMN TRANSFERS

TOWER PODIUM STRUCTURE

**WEST
ELEVATION**

THE NEW
YORK TOWER
JOINS THE MET
LIFE TOWER
AND THE
EMPIRE STATE
BUILDING ON
THE SKYLINE.

Do you think the creative process is,
in part, an attempt to find the narrative?

IF THERE WASN'T A STORY, THEN THE BUILDING WOULD JUST BE AN ABSTRACT EXERCISE, AS IF IT WERE TALKING TO ITSELF.

AN EXPAN-
SION OF THE
CULTURAL
HISTORY
MUSEUM IN
OSNABRÜCK,
THE MUSEUM
IS DEDICATED
TO THE WORK
OF FELIX
NUSSBAUM,
BORN IN THE
CITY IN 1904
AND KILLED AT
AUSCHWITZ IN
1944.

THREE VOL-
UMES IN THREE
MATERIALS—
CONCRETE,
WOOD, AND
METAL—
REPRESENT
THE LIFE AND
FATE OF FELIX
NUSSBAUM.

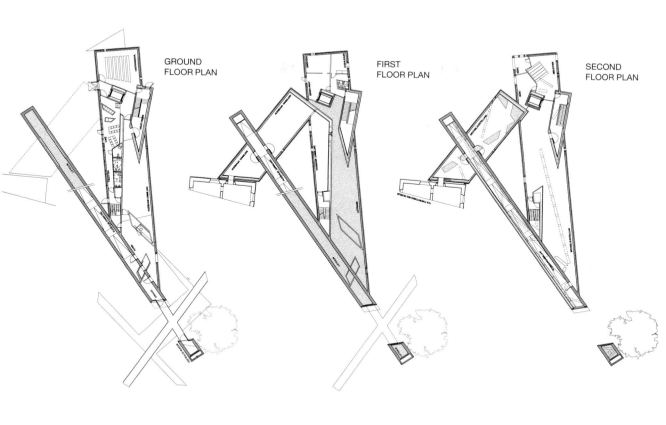

GROUND
FLOOR PLAN

FIRST
FLOOR PLAN

SECOND
FLOOR PLAN

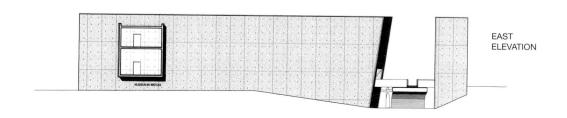

EAST
ELEVATION

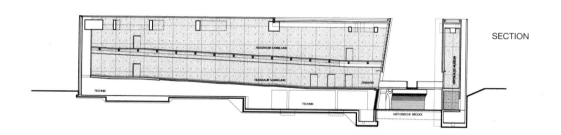

SECTION

THE MAIN
ENTRANCE TO
THE MUSEUM
IS A NARROW
DOOR INTO
A CONCRETE
VOLUME.

OFTEN
APPEARING
IN HIS PAINT-
INGS, THE
SUNFLOWER
WAS FELIX
NUSSBAUM'S
FAVORITE
FLOWER.

THE WOODEN
BUILDING
CONTAINS THE
EARLY WORKS
OF NUSSBAUM.
THE PALE
CAST OF LIGHT
HINTS AT THE
FUTURE.

THE CENTRAL SPACE OF THE MUSEUM IS A NARROW WALKWAY CONTAINING NUSSBAUM'S LAST PAINTINGS.

You've built a 9/11 memorial in Italy.
What is its connection to New York?

THE OPEN GLASS BOOK ACROSS FROM GIOTTO'S CHAPEL SUSPENDS A TWISTED AND CHARRED BEAM FROM GROUND ZERO.

THE MEMO-
RIAL TAKES
THE FORM
OF THE BOOK
OF HISTORY.
GLAZED AND
OPAQUE GLASS
AND STEEL
MEET AT THE
SPINE OF THE
BOOK.

THE AXIS
BETWEEN PADUA
AND NEW YORK
TRAVERSES
VIOLENCE AND
REFLECTION.

A TORTURED
STEEL BEAM
FROM GROUND
ZERO IS
INSERTED IN
THE GLASS
STRUCTURE
OF THE
MEMORIAL.

Even though you are building skyscrapers
all over the world, do your clients ever want them
to be like what they've seen before?

TRADITION RADI- CALLY IMBUES NEW FORMS WITH FORGOT- TEN MEANINGS. THE CREATIVE ACT REQUIRES THE INDIVIDUAL SIGNATURE.

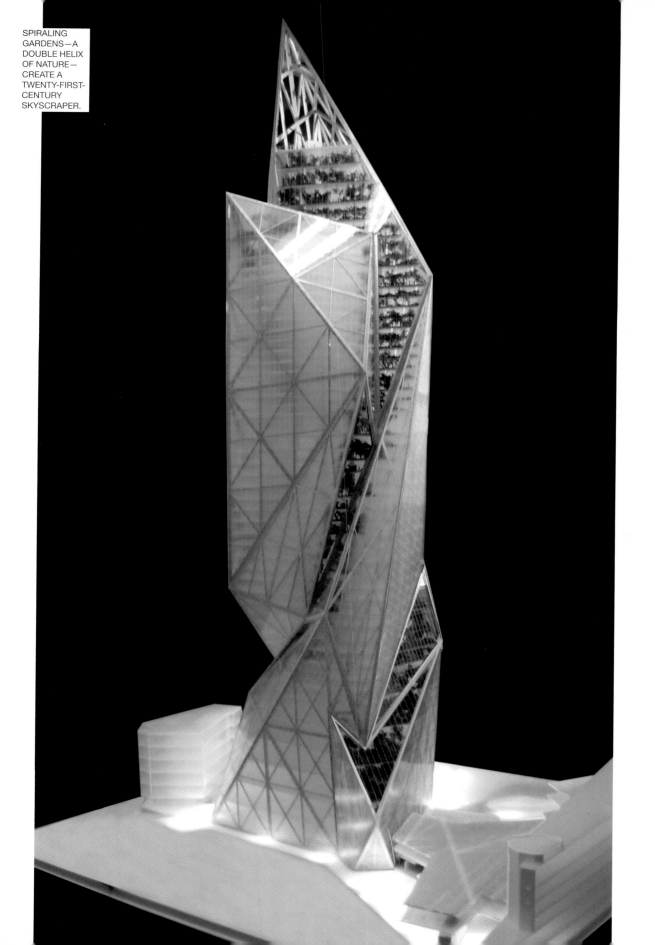

SPIRALING
GARDENS—A
DOUBLE HELIX
OF NATURE—
CREATE A
TWENTY-FIRST-
CENTURY
SKYSCRAPER.

THE FORM
OF THE
SKYSCRAPER
SIGNALS A NEW
RELATIONSHIP
TO FUNCTION,
SUSTAIN-
ABILITY, AND
THE CULTURE
OF THE
METROPOLIS.

THE BASE OF
THE BUILDING
CONNECTS
TO AN EXIST-
ING SHOPPING
CENTER
AND TO THE
SURROUND-
ING OFFICE
BUILDINGS.

THE OASIS
PROVIDES
A NEW
SPACE FOR
ENCOUNTER.

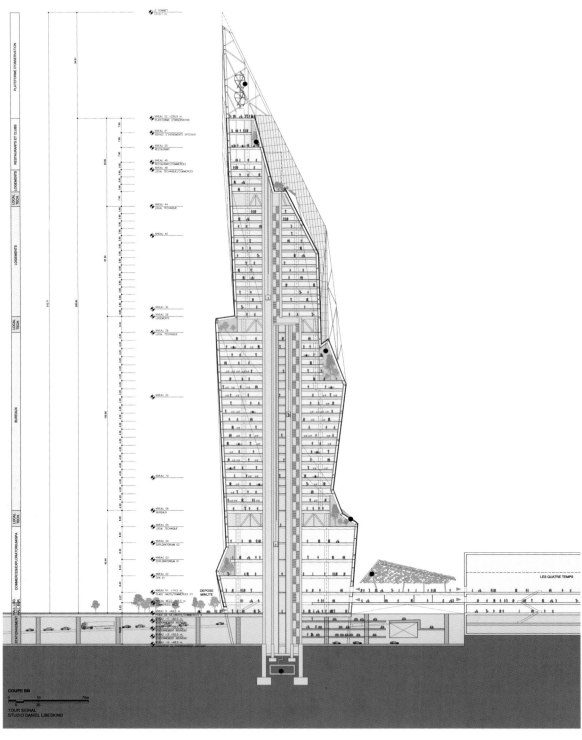

COUPE BB

TOUR SIGNAL
STUDIO DANIEL LIBESKIND

SECTION

TOUR SIGNAL
BREAKS DOWN
THE SCALE OF
CARTESIAN
SKYSCRAPERS.
LIKE A TREE, IT
IS ROOTED IN
THE GROUND
AND SHAPED
BY LIGHT.

You've had a remarkable range of work and
it seems only to broaden.

A MODEST HOUSE, A SKY-SCRAPER, A HUGE DEVELOP-MENT: HOW LUCKY TO MOVE BEYOND THEORY INTO THE COM-PLEXITY OF PRACTICE.

THE STUDIO WITH ITS SIMPLE GEOM-ETRIES STANDS ON A MAIN ROAD.

THE BUILD-
ING IS A
SCULPTURE
THAT SHOW-
CASES ART.
AN INTERNAL
LANDSCAPE
IS A VITAL ELE-
MENT OF THE
COMPOSITION.

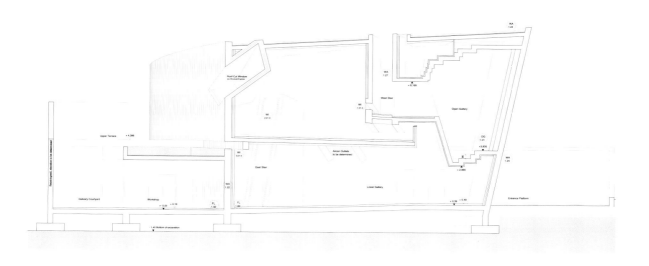

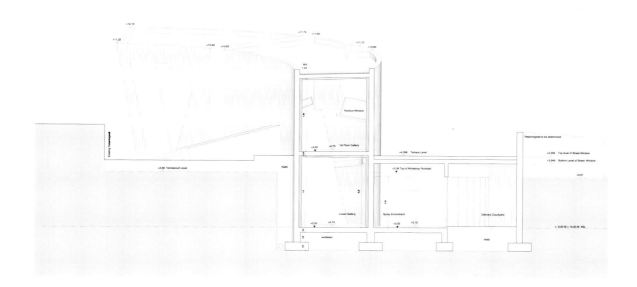

SECTIONS

THE STUDIO REINTERPRETS THE ARCHITEC-TURE OF THE MEDITERRA-NEAN REGION.

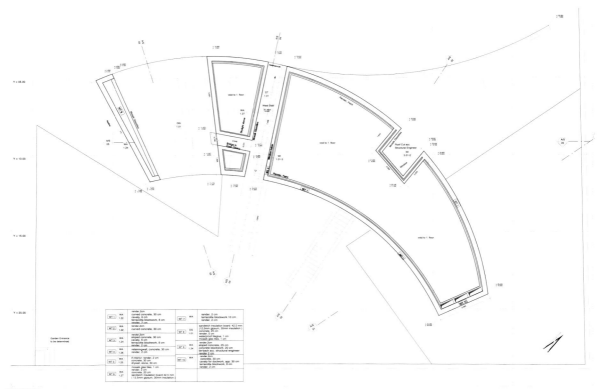

**SECOND
FLOOR PLAN**

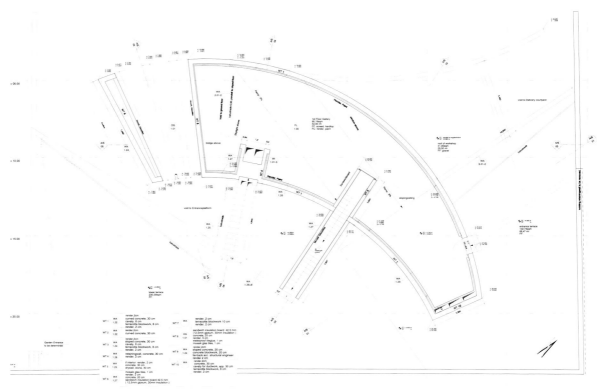

**FIRST
FLOOR PLAN**

THE TWO
STAIRS LEAD
TO TWO
DIFFERENT
DESTINATIONS.

Most prefabs are the result of a logic of containers.
How does yours differ?

THERE IS NO REASON THAT AN INDUSTRIAL PROCESS TODAY CANNOT PRO-DUCE A FREELY FORMED YET RATIONAL FIGURE

FORM, STRUC-
TURE, AND
FUNCTION
FOLLOW A
NEW IDEA OF
SUSTAINABLE
LIVING.

FLEXIBLE MOD-
ULES, UNIQUE
WINDOWS, AND
EXPRESSIVE
OUTDOOR
AREAS SHAPE
A SPACE FOR
EVERYDAY
LIVING.

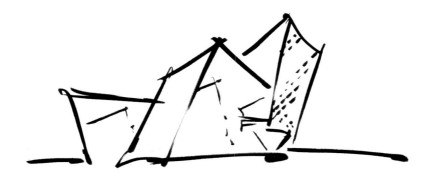

OBLIQUELY
SHAPED VOL-
UMES ALLOW
FOR ROOMS
OF UNUSUAL
HEIGHT.

How do symbols enter into your buildings?

I BELIEVE IN A SPIRITUAL SEARCH FOR THE BALANCE BETWEEN ACTIVITY AND MEDITATION, EMBODIED IN SPECIFIC SYMBOLS OF THE BUILDING.

THE WOHL CENTRE OFFERS A GOLDEN GATEWAY TO LEARNING AT BAR-ILAN UNIVERSITY.

THE ENTRANCE LOBBY CAN ACCOMMODATE EXHIBITIONS, EVENTS, AND SEMINARS.

THE AUDITO-
RIUM HOVERS
ABOVE THE
ENTRANCE
TERRACE.

THE WALLS OF
THE BUILDING
SUPPORT AND
BALANCE THE
CANTILEVERED,
BOOKLIKE
FORM OF THE
AUDITORIUM.

D   C   B   A

+14.60
EXT. TERRACE
+11.65

AUDITORIUM

+03.50

+00.34

±00.00

HALL II   MAIN LOBBY

-04.50

MECHANICAL ROOM

SECTION

+19.10

+14.60

+14.50

+08.65

D   C   B   A

THE CENTRAL
SPINE CON-
TAINS VERTICAL
CIRCULATION;
ACTS AS A
DIVIDER
BETWEEN
SEMINAR
ROOMS AND
THE CAFÉ
AND GROUND
LEVEL; AND
SUPPORTS THE
AUDITORIUM
ON THE UPPER
LEVEL.

A SYMBOLIC
LABYRINTH
GENERATES
THE SPACE
OF THE
THOUSAND-
SEAT AUDI-
TORIUM. THE
LABYRINTH IS
EXPRESSED ON
THE EXTERIOR
AS WELL.

How has the process of creating the Contemporary Jewish Museum in San Francisco, which is new, been different from working with established museums?

THE MUSEUM EXPRESSES THE CHALLENGE OF FINDING IDENTITY AMID THE DIVERSITY OF EXISTING BUILDINGS. IT CELEBRATES COMPLEXITY.

THE SYMBOLIC
FORMS OF
THE MUSEUM
BURST FROM
HISTORIC
GROUNDS.

THREE THOU-
SAND STEEL-
BLUE DIAMONDS
EMERGE INTO
THE SKY.

WITHIN THE WALLS OF A FORMER POWER SUBSTATION, BEHIND A CHURCH, AND UNDER A HOTEL, THE MUSEUM WEAVES A NEW FOCUS FOR THE NEIGH-BORHOOD. THE FORM OF THE STRUCTURE IS COMPOSED OF TWO LETTERS, THE *YUD* AND THE *CHET*, WHICH MAKE UP *CHAI*, *L'CHAIM*, TO LIFE.

THE INTERSEC-
TION BETWEEN
THE *YUD* AND
THE *CHET*
FORMS CRE-
ATES A LINK
BETWEEN THE
SHOP AND THE
MAIN STAIR.

RETRACTABLE
SEATING
OFFERS FLEX-
IBILITY TO THE
MULTIPURPOSE
AUDITORIUM.

THE HALL OF
THE SUBSTA-
TION IS VISIBLE
THROUGH THE
FORMS OF THE
NEW MUSEUM.

THE *YUD*
FORM POINTS
UPWARD.

THE *YUD* FORM CANTILEVERS INTO THE BUILDING NEXT TO THE MAIN STAIR.

THE UPPER
LEVEL OF THE
YUD FORM
HAS THIRTY-SIX
DIAMOND-
SHAPED
WINDOWS.

THE ASCENDING *CHET* FORM AND THE POWER STATION SKYLIGHTS HARMONIZE IN THE UPPER GALLERY.

THE MUSEUM IS A CONVERSATION BETWEEN THE INDUSTRIAL ARCHITECTURE OF THE POWER STATION AND THE ENERGY OF THE CULTURAL INSTITUTION.

What can you do with a modern office building that has
been started by another architect?

EVEN WITHIN THE TWO METERS AVAILABLE FOR DESIGN, I WAS ABLE TO GIVE A UNIQUE AND URBAN IDENTITY BOTH INSIDE AND OUTSIDE.

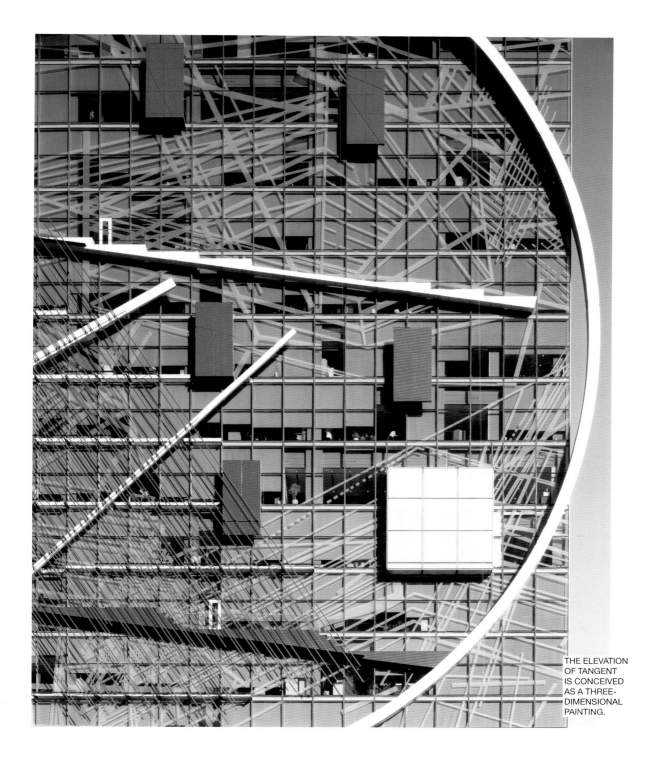

THE ELEVATION
OF TANGENT
IS CONCEIVED
AS A THREE-
DIMENSIONAL
PAINTING.

FROM INSIDE
THE BUILDING,
THE FACADE
OFFERS A
VARIETY OF
ATMOSPHERES.

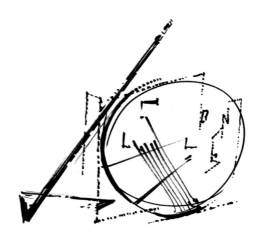

THE TANGENT LINE TRAVERSES THE BUILDING OBLIQUELY, CONNECTING THE ROOF WITH THE SUBWAY STATION BELOW.

PROJECTIONS,
SCREENS,
VERANDAS,
BALCONIES,
AND LOUVERS
OPEN THE
BUILDING TO
THE CITY.

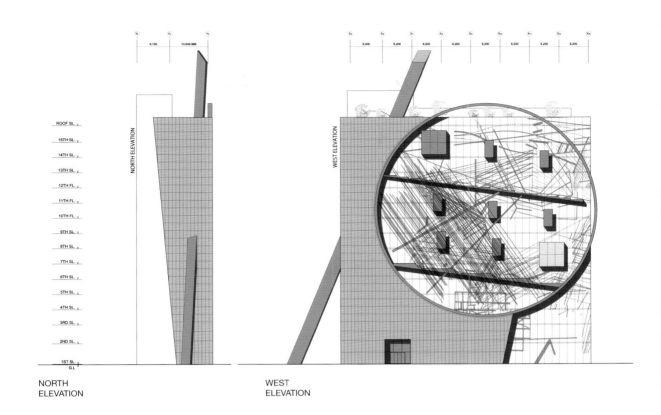

NORTH
ELEVATION

WEST
ELEVATION

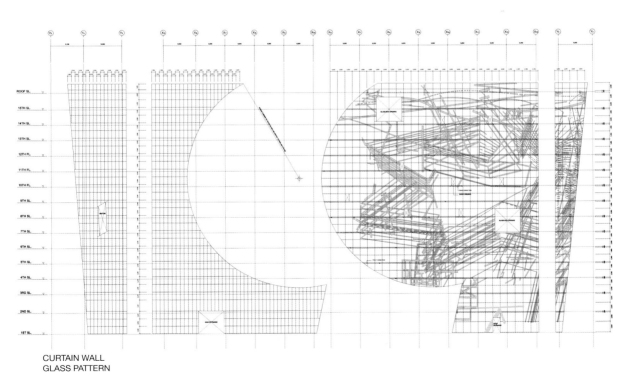

CURTAIN WALL
GLASS PATTERN

THE TANGENT
FORMS A SPIRE
ABOVE THE
ROOF GARDEN,
A PLACE OF
CALM.

DOMINATING THE FACADE IS A SIXTY-TWO-METER RING, A VIVID COMBINATION OF GRAPHIC ELEMENTS AND COLORS.

Do you still feel that you're as close to the art
of architecture as you were before?

NOW THAT MY PRACTICE IS LARGER, I FIND THAT THE SYN— ERGY BETWEEN DIFFERENT PROGRAMS OFFERS MORE BREADTH.

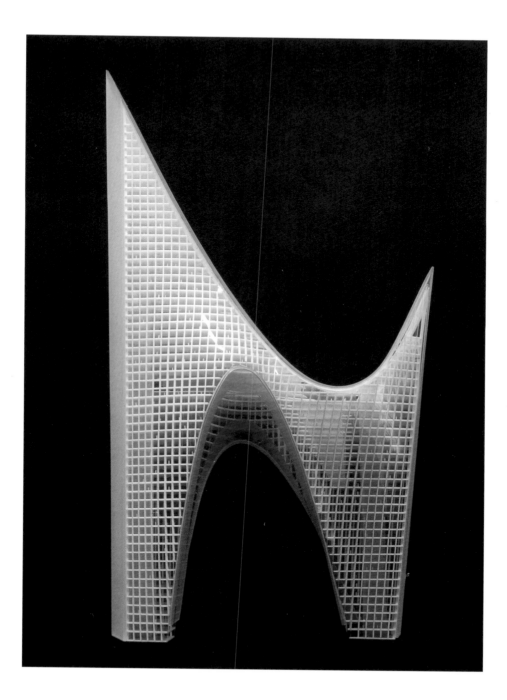

View from Kirochnaya street

"Люблю тебя, Петра творенье;
Люблю твой строгий, стройный вид,"

- ПУШКИН -

TWO TOWERS
UNITED BY
A GATEWAY
FORM A NEW
FIGURE OF A
HIGH-RISE.
THE INNER
SURFACE OF
THE ARCH
INCORPORATES
LARGE GLAZED
AREAS.

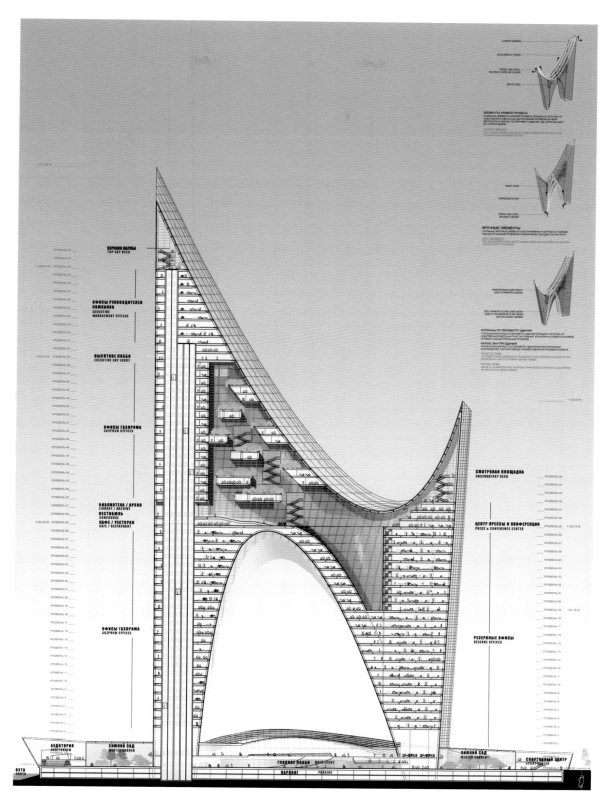

SECTION

THE FORM OF THE TOWER CONTRIBUTES TO THE SKY-LINE, COMPLE-MENTING THE SPIRES OF ST. PETERSBURG AND THE URBAN FABRIC OF THE CITY.

It was very exciting to see the connection, new and old,
in the Royal Ontario Museum, and the extent to which the
building is very much a response to the older building.

I WANTED TO BUILD DYNAMIC SPACES THAT INVITE THE VISITOR EVEN BEFORE ENTERING.

THE CRYSTALS
IN THE
MUSEUM
COLLECTION
INSPIRED THE
ADDITION.

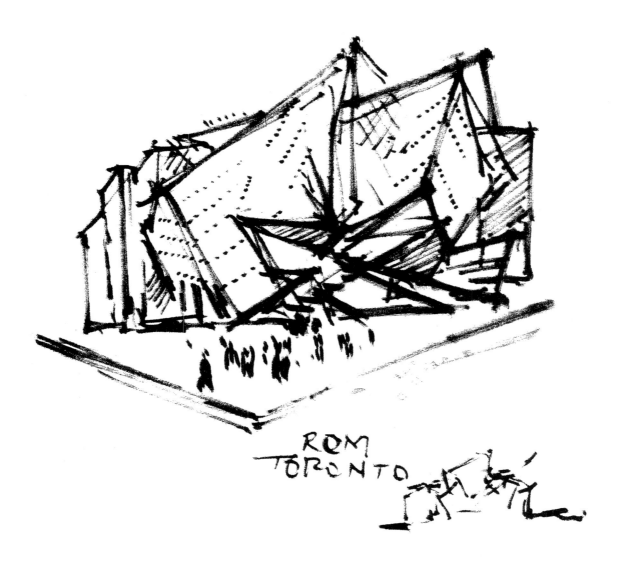

ROM
TORONTO

THE CRYSTAL TOUCHES THE HISTORIC STRUCTURE WITH CARE, HIGHLIGHTING THE IMPORTANCE OF THE INTERSECTION BETWEEN THE TWO.

THE CRYSTAL CREATES NEW ENTRANCES ON BLOOR STREET AND SHOWS OFF THE COLLECTION THROUGH GIGANTIC WINDOWS. THE GEOMETRY OF THE STRUCTURE ENSURES THAT EACH FACET TAKES ON A DIFFERENT COLOR.

THE INTERSEC-
TION BETWEEN
THE LARGE
FORMS CRE-
ATES A SPACE
OF TRANSI-
TION; LIGHT
AND SOUND
EVENTS TAKE
PLACE IN THIS
AREA.

A WALL DAT-
ING TO 1914
FORMS THE
BACKDROP
FOR A LARGE
EVENT SPACE.
TWO SKY-
LIGHTS TAKE
THE FORM OF
CRYSTALS.

THE CRYSTAL CHAIRS ARE A MICROCOSM OF THE BUILDING.

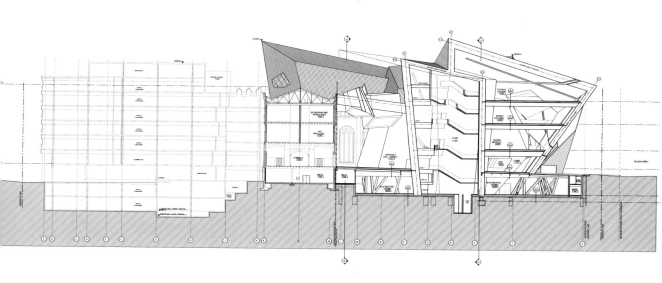

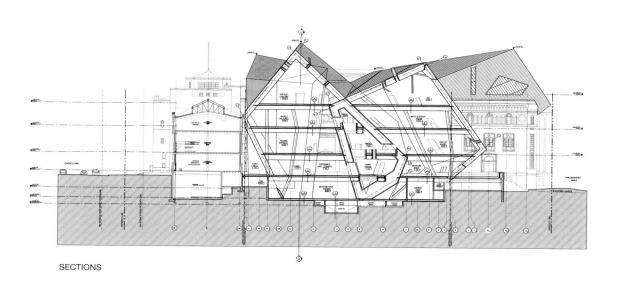

SECTIONS

Your building in Toronto has a different
sort of form—it curves at the top—and a very
different kind of skin as well.

THE TOWER IS AN URBAN SCULPTURE COMBINING CULTURE AND RESIDENCES IN A DRAMATIC AND SWEEPING GESTURE.

IN ADDITION TO
THE HISTORIC
HUMMINGBIRD
THEATRE,
THE L TOWER
INCLUDES A
NEW ARTS AND
CULTURAL
FACILITY AND
A RESIDENTIAL
TOWER. THE
BASE OF THE
BUILDING
OPENS TO
CREATE A
LIVELY PLAZA.

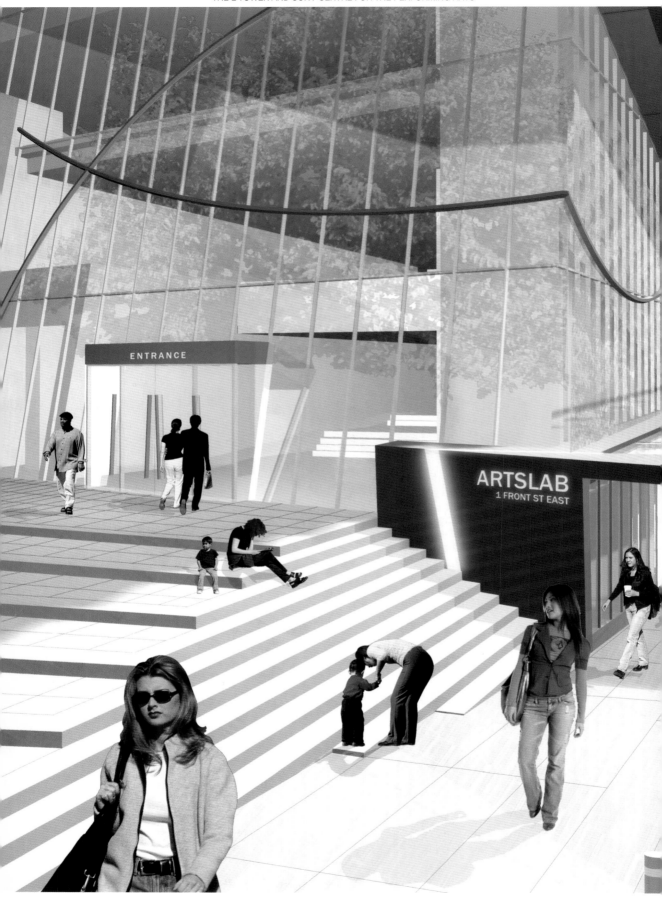

THE TOWER
BASE AND
THE MAIN
ENTRANCE
MODULATE THE
STREETSCAPE,
PROVIDING
A SCALE TO
PEDESTRIAN
ACTIVITY.

SECTION

You have referred to yourself as "always still retaining a little bit of naiveté."
I don't know any other architect who would admit to that.

NAIVETÉ IS REMAINING OPEN TO NEW AND UNEXPECTED IDEAS. I LIKE TO QUESTION THE OBVIOUS.

AN EXPRES-
SIVE CIVIC
BUILDING, THE
HERMITAGE-
GUGGENHEIM
RESTORES
TO VILNIUS
ITS PRE–
WORLD WAR II
CULTURAL
VIBRANCY.

THE SWEEP-
ING ARCS OF
THE MUSEUM
EMBRACE OLD
AND NEW.

A PUBLIC PLAZA AT THE MUSEUM ENTRANCE IS A NEW DESTINATION IN A NETWORK OF REVITALIZED GREEN SPACES. WITHIN THE ASCENDING HYPERBOLIC VOLUME IS A RESTAURANT WITH PANORAMIC VIEWS OF THE HISTORIC CITY.

THE INTERIOR SPACES CASCADE INTO A LANDSCAPE WITHIN THE BUILDING.

THE CON-
TOURS OF
THE BUILDING
APPEAR TO
HAVE BEEN
CREATED BY
THE NERIS
RIVER.

HERMITAGE-GUGGENHEIM VILNIUS MUSEUM

**WEST
ELEVATION**

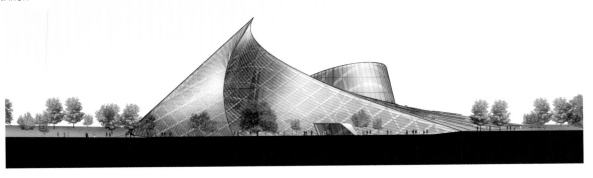

**EAST
ELEVATION**

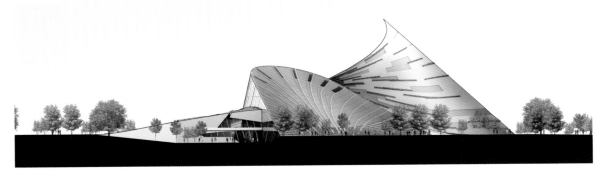

**SOUTH
ELEVATION**

**NORTH
ELEVATION**

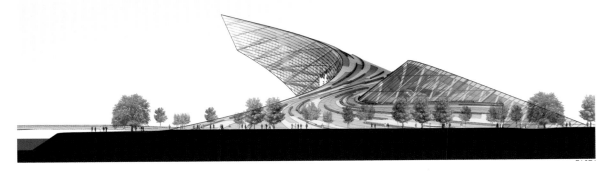

Labels within image:
WALKING PATHS
POOLS
SERVICE VEHICLE ENTRANCE
OUTDOOR AMPHITHEATER
THEATER PLAZA
NEW TERRACE PLAZA
NERIS
EXISTING PEDESTRIAN BRIDGE
ENTRY PLAZA
RIVER PARK
RIVER

SITE PLAN

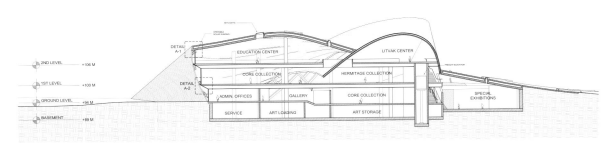

2ND LEVEL +106 M	EDUCATION CENTER	LITVAK CENTER	
1ST LEVEL +100 M	CORE COLLECTION	HERMITAGE COLLECTION	
GROUND LEVEL +94 M	ADMIN. OFFICES	GALLERY	CORE COLLECTION	SPECIAL EXHIBITIONS
BASEMENT +89 M	SERVICE	ART LOADING	ART STORAGE	

DETAIL A-1

DETAIL A-2

SECTIONS

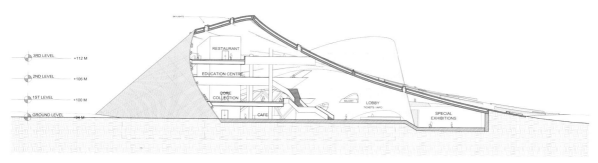

How did you derive the form for
your mixed-use building in Warsaw?

THE BUILDING STANDS ACROSS FROM THE STALINIST PALACE OF CULTURE. I WANTED THE POLISH EAGLE TO SOAR ONCE AGAIN OVER WARSAW.

STALIN'S
PALACE OF
CULTURE
AND SCIENCE
NO LONGER
DOMINATES
THE WARSAW
SKYLINE.

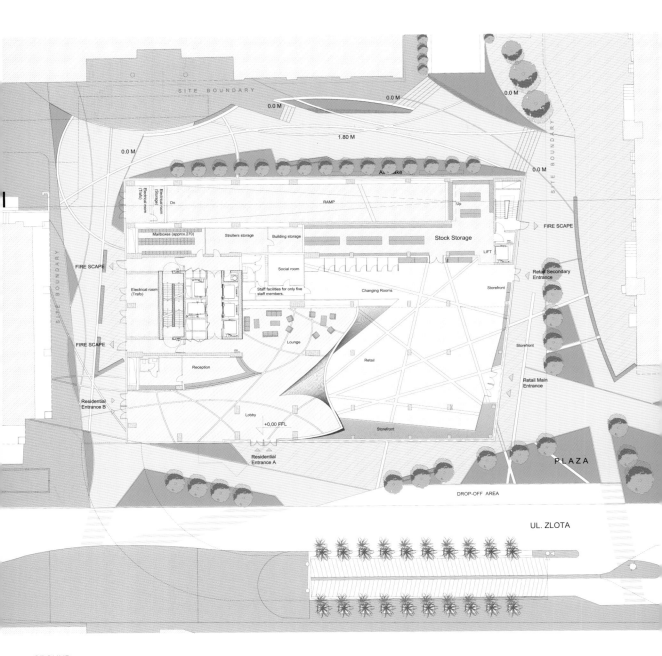

GROUND
PLAN

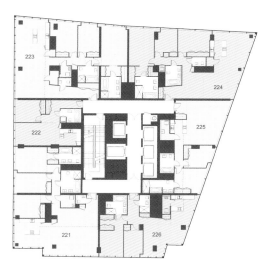

MIDDLE
FLOOR PLAN

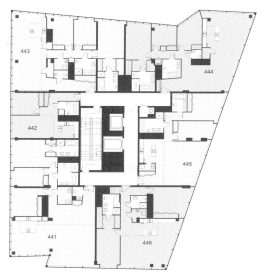

UPPER
FLOOR PLAN

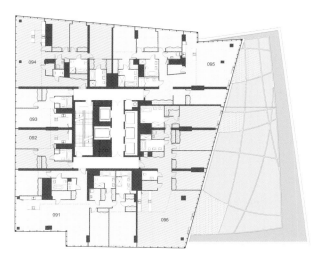

LOWER
FLOOR PLAN

AN UPPER-LEVEL SPA AND A GROUND-LEVEL ENTRANCE LOBBY ARE TWO OF THE SHARED PUBLIC SPACES.

FLOOR PLANS
TAKE ACCOUNT
OF NEIGHBORS
AND OFFER
ICONIC VIEWS
OF WARSAW.

THE WINGLIKE FORM IS AN ENERGETIC EXPRESSION OF FREEDOM.

PROJECT CREDITS

Jewish Museum Berlin
Berlin, Germany, 1999
Client: Stiftung Jüdisches Museum Berlin
Project Team Leaders: Matthias Reese, Jan Dinnebier,
Stefan Blach
Competition Team: Attilio Terragni, Marina Stankovic,
Marco Vido, Donald Bates
Design Team: Tarla MacGabhann, Noel McCauley,
Claudia Reisenberger, Eric J. Schall, Solveig Scheper, Ilkka
Tarkanen, Anne Marie O'Connor,
Bernhard von Hammerstein, David Hunter,
Gerhard Brun, Thomas Willemeit
Cost and Site Supervision: Lubic & Woehrlin
Structural Engineer: GSE Tragwerkplaner,
IGW Ingenieurgruppe Wiese
Mechanical/Electrical/Plumbing Engineer:
Klimasystemtechnik
Civil Engineer: Cziesielski & Partner
Landscape Architect: Müller, Knippschild, Wehberg
Lighting Designer: Lichtplanung Dinnebier
Raw Construction: Fischer Bau
Windows: Trube & Kings
Facade: Werner & Sohn
Mechanical Systems: Klimabau, Voigt Bode, Nordbau
Electrical Systems: Alpha
Glass Courtyard, 2007
Client: Jewish Museum Berlin
Principal: Stefan Blach
Design Team: Arnault Biou, Gerhard Brun
Architect of Record: Reese Architekten
Cost and Site Supervision: Lubic & Woehrlin
Structural Engineer: GSE Ingenieur-Gesellschaft
Mechanical/Electrical/Plumbing Engineer: Clean Room Consulting
Facade Consultant: ARUP (Berlin)
Lighting Designer: Studio Dinnebier
Raw Construction: Markische Ingenieur Bau
Steel: Rudolstädter Systembau
Glazing System: FSB Freienhufener

Editoriale Bresciana Tower
Brescia, Italy, 2010
Client: Editoriale Bresciana
Principal: Yama Karim
Competition Team: Carla Swickerath, Jason Jimenez, David
Stockwell
Design Team: Attilio Terragni, Luca Mangione, Lucia Bazzoli,
Marta Oddone, Maddelena Beretta, Sergey Belov, Agostino
Ghirardelli
Joint Venture Partner: CityEdge
Cost Control: Sviluppo Sistema Fiera
Structural/Civil Engineer, Site Control: Tecne
Mechanical/Electrical/Plumbing Engineer: Manens Intertecnica
Urban Planning Management: Cadeo Architettura

Westside Shopping and Leisure Center
Brunnen, Switzerland, 2008
Client: Neue Brünnen, Genossenschaft Migros Aare
Design Team Leader: Barbara Holzer
Design Team: Jochen Klein, Birgit Rieder, Stefan Zopp, Guillaume
Chapallaz, Attilio Lavezzari, Philip Peterson,
Ka Wing Lo, Ina Hesselmann, Jens Hoffmann,
Jean-Lucien Gay, Stephanie Tippmann, Bianca Baumgart,
Marian Chabrera, Thomas Deuble, Gerrit Grigoleit, Michael Heim,
Mauricio Martins, Emil Muenger,
Julia Voormann, Nicolas Rossier, Roberto Forte,
Ross Anderson, Stephane Carnuccini, Sidsel Kromann,
Vaugn Borlund, Hans-Adam Weibel, Stefan Kiener, Gerhard Brun
Joint Venture Partners: Architekt Daniel Libeskind with
Burckhardt + Partner

Project Management: Sulzer + Buzzi Baumanagement
Structural Engineer: B+S Ingenieur, Bächtold & Moor
Mechanical/Electrical Engineer: Kannewischer Ingenieurbüro
Mechanical Engineer: Enerconom, Kannewischer Ingenieurbüro
Electrical/Lighting Engineer: Hefti. Hess. Martignoni. Elektro
Landscape Architect: 4d Landschaftsarchitekten, Weber +
Brönnimann
Facade Consultant: Emmer Pfenninger Partner, SJB.Kempter.
Fitze
Fire Protection Consultant: Christian Wälchli
Building Physics: Zeugin Bauberatungen
Contractor: ARGE TU Westside, Rhomberg Bau, Strabag,
Rolf Derrer

Haeundae Udong Hyundai I'Park
Busan, South Korea, 2011
Client: Hyundai Development Company
Principal: Carla Swickerath
Design Team: Seungki Min, Ching-Wen Lin, Byungdon Yoo,
Joy Cardillo, Kee Lew, Sarah Nichols, Jared Olmsted,
Ian Gordon, Jan Kaluza, Injune Kim, Naser Madouh, Gerhard
Brun, Jean-Lucien Gay, Emily Wells, Taek Kim
Architect of Record: Kunwon, Hanmi
Structural Engineer: ARUP (New York), Dong Yang Structural
Engineers Co.
Mechanical/Electrical/Plumbing Engineer: Syska Hennessy,
Hyun Woo Mechanical Engineering
Geotechnical Engineer: Saegil E & C Co.
Landscape Consultant: Ctopos
Curtain Wall Consultant: Wallplus
Fire Protection Consultant: Yung-Do Engineering Co.
Lighting Consultant: LPA
Contractor: Hyundai Development Company

Danish Jewish Museum
Copenhagen, Denmark, 2003
Client: The Danish Jewish Museum
Design Team Leader: Susanne Milne
Design Team: Shawn Duffee, Wendy James, Stefan Blach
Renovation of Galejhuset: Fogh & Følner Arkitektfirma
Consulting Engineer: Hansen & Henneberg
Structural Engineer: Moe & Brødsgaard
Mechanical/Electrical Engineer: Moe & Brødsgaard
Landscape Consultant: GHB Landskabsarkitekter
Exhibition Designer: Kvorning Design & Kommunikation
Contractor: Tomrerfirma Gert Fogt

The Ascent at Roebling's Bridge
Covington, Kentucky, 2008
Client: Corporex
Principal: Yama Karim
Design Team: Amanda Short, Joe Rom, David Stockwell, Jason
Jimenez, Wendy James
Architect of Record: GBBN Architects
Structural Engineer: THP Limited
Mechanical/Electrical/Plumbing Engineer: KLH Engineering
Contractor: Dugan & Meyers Construction

Extension to the Denver Art Museum, Frederic C.
Hamilton Building
Denver, Colorado, 2006
Client: The Denver Art Museum; City of Denver, Colorado
Principals: Arne Emerson, Stefan Blach
Competition Team: Rob Claiborne, Wolfgang Gollwitzer, Thore
Garbers, Guadalupe Cantu, Carla Swickerath, Jason Scroggin
Design Team: Rob Claiborne, Guadalupe Cantu, Anthony Neff,
Sid Conn, Daniel Richmond, Mazie Huh
Joint Venture Partner: Davis Partnership
Structural Engineer: ARUP (Los Angeles)
Structural Connection Design: Structural Consultants
Mechanical Air: ARUP

Mechanical/Electrical Engineer: MKK Engineers
Civil Engineer: J. F. Sato and Associates
Landscape Architect: Studio Daniel Libeskind with Davis
Partnership
Facade Consultant: ARUP
Lighting Consultant: George Sexton and Associates
Theater Consultant: Auerbach Pollack Friedlander
Contractor: M. A. Mortensen Co.

Denver Art Museum Residences
Denver, Colorado, 2006
Client: Mile High Development, Corporex
Principal: Arne Emerson
Design Team: Mazie Huh, Anthony Neff, Robert Arens
Joint Venture Partner: Davis Partnership
Structural Engineer: Jirsa Hedrick & Associates
Mechanical Design Consultant (for AMI Mechanical): DMCE
Engineering
Civil Engineer: J. F. Sato and Associates
Landscape Architect: Studio Daniel Libeskind with Davis
Partnership
Interior Designer: Studio Daniel Libeskind with Davis Partnership
Contractor: Milender White Construction Co.
Design-Build Mechanical Contractor: AMI Mechanical
Design-Build Electrical Contractor: Ludvik Electric

Military History Museum
Dresden, Germany, 2009
Client: BMVG Bundesministerium der Verteidigung
Design Team Leader: Jochen Klein
Design Team: Peter Haubert, Guillaume Chapallaz, Marcel Nette,
Ka Wing Lo, Helko Rettschlag, Ina Hesselmann
Joint Venture Partner: Architekt Daniel Libeskind
Cost and Site Supervision: Lubic & Woehrlin
Structural Engineer: GSE Ingenieur-Gesellschaft
Mechanical/Electrical Engineer: Ipro Industrieprojektierung
Civil Engineer: Arnold Consult
Auditing Statics: Ing. Consult Cornelius-Schwarz-Zeitler
Landscape Architect: Volker von Gagern
Fire Protection Consultant: Ingenieurbüro Heilmann
Lighting Designer: Delux
Exhibition Designer: H. G. Merz with Holzer Kobler Architekturen
Demolition: Bertram für Bau und Gewerbe
Foundation, Steel Beams: Firma Bauer Spezialtiefbau
Raw Construction: Hentschke Bau
Steel Construction, Wedge: Gerhard Schilling Stahlbau und
Montage
Steel Construction, Floor Plates: Stahlbau Verbundträger
Facade Contractor: Josef Gartner

Grand Canal Square Theatre and Commercial Development
Dublin, Ireland, 2009
Client: Ramford
Principal: Stefan Blach
Design Team Leader: Gerhard Brun
Design Team: Patrick Cox, Toralf Sümmchen,
Andreas Baumgärtner, Matthias Rühl, Phil Binkert,
Guillaume Chapallaz, Niels Fehlig, Katja Rinderspacher,
Julia Bauer, Jean-Lucien Gay, Kaori Hirasawa,
Jens Jessen, Maja Leonelli, Luca Mangione, Nathaniel
Lloyd, Joanna Pytlik
Joint Venture Partner: Architekt Daniel Libeskind
Architect of Record: McCauley Daye O'Connell Architects
Project Management: Lafferty Project Management
Structural Engineer: ARUP (Dublin)
Mechanical/Electrical/Plumbing Engineer: ARUP
Venue and Acoustic Consultant: ARUP
Facade Consultant: Billings Design Associates
Cladding Consultant, Offices and Theater BOH Facade:
Permasteelisa Group
Cladding Consultant, Theater Stainless-Steel Facade,

FOH Curtain Steel/Glass: Permasteelisa Central Europe
Fire Protection Consultant: Michael Slattery & Associates
Lighting Designer: Pritchard Themis
Health and Safety: Bruce Shaw Partnership
Cost Estimation: Davis Langdon
Main Contractor, Raw Construction: John Sisk & Son

Roedingsmarkt
Hamburg, Germany, 2011
Client: DWI Gruppe Hamburg
Principal: Stefan Blach
Design Team: Brian Melcher, Sascha Manteufel, Brian McIntosh,
Elan Lipson, Gen Kato, Jerry Figurski, Thunyalux Hiransaroj,
Matthew Young
Structural Engineer: Dröge • Baade • Nagaraj

Creative Media Center
Hong Kong, 2010
Client: City University of Hong Kong
Principals: Eric Sutherland, Wendy James
Competition Team: Martin Ostermann, Simon Dittmann, Philipp
Utermoehl, Gerhard Brun, Michael Brown,
Bahadir Parali
Design Team: Joy Cardillo, Ka Wing Lo, Sean Ellis, Laphan Fan,
Susanne Milne, Tomoro Aida, Taek Kim, Donald Shillingburg,
Sarah Nichols, Jennifer Russell
Joint Venture Partner: Leigh & Orange
Structural Engineer: ARUP (London/Hong Kong)
Mechanical/Electrical/Plumbing Engineer: ARUP
Geotechnical/Civil Engineer: ARUP
Landscape Architect: ADI Limited
Facade Consultant: ARUP
Fire Protection Consultant: ARUP
Lighting Designer: ARUP
IT and Communications, Audiovisual, Acoustics: ARUP
Site Formation: Kaden Construction Co.
Town Planning: EDAW
Cost Estimation: Levett and Bailey
Contractor: China Resources Construction

Riverstone
Incheon, South Korea, 2013
Client: Gale International
Retail Developer: Taubman Asia Limited
Principal: Arne Emerson
Design Team: Jaehong Jay Kim, Hyung Seung Min, Jennifer
Russell, Seung Ra, Katja Rinderspacher, Ka-Yeon Lee,
Ian Gordon, Sean Ellis, Gen Kato, Petra Lindfors
Architect of Record: Baum Architects
Structural Engineer: ARUP (New York), Dawon
Mechanical/Electrical/Plumbing Engineer: Cosentini Associates,
Woowon
Acoustical Engineer: ARUP
Landscape Architect: Vonder Design
Facade Consultant: ALT Limited
Interior Designer: Studio Daniel Libeskind with Benoy
Lighting Designer: ARUP
Food Court Designer: MBBD
Ice Rink Show Designer: Thinkwell
Retail Planning Consultant: BKBC Architects
Cost Estimation: DLS, Faithful + Gould
Ice Rink Contractor: CIMCO

Jerusalem Oriya
Jerusalem, Israel, 2010
Client: American Colony
Principal: Eric Sutherland
Design Team: Sean Ellis, Luca Ruggeri, Brandon Padron,
Ka-Yeon Lee
Architect of Record: Ranni Ziss Architects
Structural Engineer: Zvi Hemley

Landscape Designer: Tzurnamel Turner
Traffic Consultant: Michael Nakman

Reflections
Keppel Bay, Singapore, 2011
Client: Keppel Land
Principal: Yama Karim
Design Team: Arnault Biou, Seungki Min, Patrick Head, Ilana Altman, Jennifer Milliron, Vicky Lam, Bora Temelkuran, Maxi Spina, Raul Correa-Smith, Casey Miller, Josh Draper
Architect of Record: DCA Architects
Project Management: Keppel Land
Structural Engineer: T. Y. Lin International
Mechanical/Electrical/Plumbing Engineer: Beca Carter Hollings & Ferner
Civil Engineer: T. Y. Lin International
Landscape Architect: Hargreaves Associates, Sitetectonix
Curtain Wall Consultant: R. A. Heintges & Associates
Lighting Designer: LPA
Contractor: Who Hup

MGM Mirage CityCenter
Las Vegas, Nevada, 2009
Client: MGM Mirage
Principal: Carla Swickerath
Design Team: Gerhard Brun, David Stockwell, Johan van Lierop, Noah Wadden, Steven Haardt, Sean Ellis, Taek Kim, Kiwoo Park
Architect of Record: Adamson Associates Architects
Structural Engineer: Halcrow Yolles
Mechanical/Electrical/Plumbing Engineer: Flack + Kurtz
Facade Consultant: Israel Berger & Associates
Interior Designer: Rockwell Group
Lighting Designer: Focus Lighting
Collaborating Architects: Foster and Partners, Gensler, Murphy Jahn Architects, KPF, Pelli Clarke Pelli Architects, HKS, Leo A. Daly, RV Architecture
Contractor: Perini Building Company

London Metropolitan University Graduate Centre
London, England, 2004
Client: London Metropolitan University
Principal: Wendy James
Design Team: Jean-Lucien Gay, Chad Machen, Robert Hirschfield, Anne Markey
Project Management, Planning Supervision: Robinson Low Francis
Structural Engineer: Cadogan Tietz
Mechanical/Electrical/Plumbing Engineer: WSP Group
Cost Estimation: Gleeds
Contractor: Costain

Extension to the Victoria and Albert Museum
London, England, 1996
Client: The Victoria and Albert Museum
Principal: Wendy James
Competition Team: Yama Karim, Ditmar Leyk, Kimmo Friman, Lars Gräbner, Lucas Steiner
Design Team: Stefan Blach, Johannes Hucke, Jan Dinnebier, Manuel Herz, Florian Köhl, Susanne Milne, Franziska Streb, Thore Garbers
Structural Engineer: ARUP (London)
Mechanical/Electrical/Plumbing Engineer: ARUP
Cost Estimation: Gardiner & Theobald

Imperial War Museum North
Manchester, England, 2001
Client: Imperial War Museum North
Principal: Wendy James
Competition Team: Todd Rohe, Yama Karim, Lars Gräbner, Robert Slinger, Florian Köhl
Design Team: Stefan Blach, Martin Ostermann, Markus Arne,

Gerhard Brun, Chris Duisburg, Susanne Milne, Jeanette Kuo, Franziska Streb, Lars Gräbner, Soren Bisgard
Association with Architect of Record: Leach Rhodes Walker
Project Management: Gardiner & Theobald
Structural Engineer: ARUP (London/Manchester)
Mechanical Engineer: Mott MacDonald
Planning Supervisor: Gleeds
Exhibition Designer: Event, Real Studios
Cost Estimation: Turner & Townsend
Construction Management Fit Out: Interior
Contractor: Sir Robert McAlpine

Fiera Milano
Milan, Italy, 2014
Client: CityLife
Principal: Yama Karim
Competition Team: Joe Rom, Omar Toro, Terra Krieger, Josh McKeown, Ghiora Aharoni, Michael Heim, Susanne Milne
Design Team: Attilio Terragni, Agostino Ghirardelli, Chiara Assanelli, Patrick Head, Luca Mangione, Giuseppe Blengini, Amanda Short, Jonathan Fournier, Bora Temelkuran, Maddalena Beretta, Guglielmo De'Giusti, Marta Oddone, Lucia Bazzoli, Emil Muenger, Martina Valcamonica, Valentina Ruta, Anna Del Nero
Joint Venture Partner: CityEdge
Mechanical/Electrical/Plumbing Consultants: Alpina
Structural Engineer, Tower and Museum: ARUP (New York)
Mechanical/Electrical/Plumbing Engineer, Tower and Museum: ARUP
Structural Engineer, Residential: AMIS
Mechanical/Electrical/Plumbing Engineer, Residential: Manens Intertecnica
Landscape Architect: Sophie Agata Ambroise
Client Representative: Europrogetti
Collaborating Architects: Zaha Hadid Architects, Arata Isozaki & Associates, Pier Paolo Maggiora

18.36.54
New Milford, Connecticut, 2009
Client: Private
Principal: Arne Emerson
Design Team: David Stockwell, Jerry Figurski, Roy Oei
Structural Engineer: Hage Engineering
Mechanical Engineer: P. A. Collins
Civil Engineer: CCA
Lighting Designer: ARUP Lighting
Windows: Steel Windows and Doors USA
Building Science Consultant: Simpson Gumpertz & Heger
Contractor: CN Renovation Co.
Facade Contractor: A. Zahner Company

Memory Foundations
New York, New York, 2013
Client: The Port Authority of New York and New Jersey;
Lower Manhattan Development Corporation
Principal: Carla Swickerath
Competition Team: Stefan Blach, Rob Claiborne, Johannes Hucke, Michael Brown, Gerhard Brun, Jean-Lucien Gay, Martin Ostermann, Susanne Milne, Robert Arens, Sascha Manteufel, Franziska Streb, Robert Hirschfield, Philipp Utermoehl, Simon Dittmann, Alvin Sewe, Jens Hoffman, Rob Updegrafff, Yuri Fujii, Ross Anderson, Stephane Carnuccini, Chad Machen, Elliott March, Bahadir Parali, Jose Francisco Salmeron, Scott Specht, Gary Hack
Design Team: Stefan Blach, Yama Karim, Brit Probst, Gerhard Brun, Michael Brown, Joe Rom, David Stockwell, Edward Wagner, Terra Krieger, Josh McKeown, Robert Arens, Taek Kim, Omar Toro, Kevin Teague, Erik Okland, Joe Lear, Jaehong Jay Kim, Scott Friedman, Michelle Wagner, Lance Klein, Melanie Klein
Collaborating Architects: Michael Arad and Peter Walker (Reflecting Absence), Skidmore, Owings & Merrill (Freedom

Tower), Foster and Partners (Tower 2), Maki and Associates (Tower 3), Richard Rogers Partnership (Tower 4), Santiago Calatrava (Transportation Hub), Snøhetta (Visitor Orientation and Education Center)

New York Tower
New York, New York, 2012
Client: Elad Properties
Principal: Yama Karim
Design Team: Joe Rom, Brian Melcher, Jonathan Fournier, Sergey Belov
Architect of Record: Costas Kondylis & Partners
Structural Engineer: WSP Cantor Seinuk
Mechanical/Electrical/Plumbing Engineer: Cosentini Associates
Subway Consultant: Stantec

Felix Nussbaum Haus
Osnabrück, Germany, 1998
Client: Stadt Osnabrück
Project Team Leaders: Barbara Holzer, Markus Aerni
Competition Team: Robert Claiborne, Sang Lee, Dietmar Leyk
Design Team: Lars Gräbner, Ariel Huber, Anne-Marie O'Connor, Claire Karsenty
Architect of Record: Reinders & Partner
Structural Engineer: Watermann
Mechanical Engineer: Jäger & Partner, Beratende Ingenieure
Landscape Architect: Müller, Knippschild, Wehberg
Lighting Designer: Dinnebier Licht
Contractor: Reinders & Partner

Memoria e Luce
Padua, Italy, 2005
Client: Regione del Veneto
Design Team: Jean-Lucien Gay, Attilio Terragni, Phil Binkert, Luca Mangione
Structural Engineer: AMIS
Lighting Designer: iGuzzini
Contractor: Permasteelisa Italy

Tour Signal, La Défense
Paris, France, 2008
Client: Orco Property Group
Principal: Carla Swickerath
Competition Team: Stephane Raymond, Johan van Lierop, Noah Wadden, Steven Haardt, Philip Mana, Injune Kim
Local Architect: Studios Architecture, SRA
Urban Design Consultant: L'Auc
Structural Engineer: ARUP (New York), Setec
Mechanical/Electrical/Plumbing Engineer: ARUP, Setec
Landscape Architect: Hargreaves Associates
Facade Consultant: ARUP, Setec
Lighting Designer: Grandeur Nature
Urban Accessibility: Systematica

Studio Weil
Port d'Andratx, Spain, 2003
Client: Barbara Weil
Principal: Wendy James
Design Team: Johannes Hucke, Mike McKay, Lars Grabner, Solveig Scheper, Thore Garbers, Jens Hoffman
Joint Venture Partner: Jaime Vidal Contesi
Structural Engineer: Adolfo Alonso Dura, Gracia Lopez Pationo
Lighting Designer: Studio Dinnebier
Contractor: Goccisa

Proportion
2008
Client: Proportion
Principal: Yama Karim

Design Team: Joe Rom, Sergey Belov
Pre-Construction Services: Rheinzink

The Wohl Centre
Ramat Gan, Israel, 2005
Client: Bar-Ilan University, Maurice Wohl Foundation
Principal: Stefan Blach
Design Team: Gerhard Brun, Michael Brown, Marian Chabrera, Robert Hirschfield, Thomas Willemeit
Architect of Record: TheHeder Architecture
Project Management: Vinko Yeeffet
Structural Engineer: Josef Kahan & Partners
Mechanical/Sanitary Engineer: Ben-Zvi Consulting Engineers
Electrical Engineer: Shalom Ozer
Acoustical Engineer: Abraham Melzer and Uzi Livni
Safety and Fire Protection Consultant: Shmuel Netanel Eng. Consultants
Lighting Consultant: Dinnebier Licht
Theater Consultant: Braslavi Architects
Waterproofing Consultant: Michael Morton Eng.
Air Conditioning and Sanitary Engineer: Moshe Ben Zvi Consulting Eng.
Cost Estimation: Eli Golding
Contractor: Ortam Sahar

The Contemporary Jewish Museum
San Francisco, California, 2008
Client: The Contemporary Jewish Museum
Principal: Carla Swickerath
Design Team: Michael Brown, Joe Rom, Michael Vanreusel, Sascha Manteufel, Omar Toro
Association with Architect of Record: WRNS Studio
Project Management: KPM Consulting
Structural Engineer: ARUP (Los Angeles), OLMM Consulting Engineers
Mechanical and Plumbing Engineer: Ajmani & Pamidi
Electrical Engineer: Silverman & Light
Lighting Designer: Auerbach Glasow French
IT Consultant: Telecom Design Group
Historic Preservation Consultant: Architectural Resources Group
Contractor: Plant Construction
Facade Contractor: A. Zahner Company

Tangent
Seoul, South Korea, 2005
Client: Hyundai Development Corporation
Principal: Stefan Blach
Design Team: Eric Sutherland, Michael Heim, Tomoro Aida
Association of Record: Himma Architecture Studio
Facade Consultant: ARUP (New York)
Interior Designer: Super Potato
Lighting Designer: LPA Lighting Planners Associates
Contractor: Hyundai Development Company

Gazprom Headquarters
St. Petersburg, Russia, 2006
Client: Gazprom
Principal: Yama Karim
Competition Team: Brian Melcher, Agostino Ghirardelli, Brandon Padron, Marco Folke Testa, Hyung Seung Min, David Jackowski
Structural Engineer: ARUP (New York)
Mechanical/Electrical/Plumbing Engineer: ARUP

Royal Ontario Museum
Toronto, Canada, 2007
Client: Royal Ontario Museum
Principal: Wendy James
Design Team: Stephane Raymond, Arne Emerson, Wan-Chi Chang, Patrick Cox, Thore Garbers, Daniel Kruger, Nathaniel Lloyd, Anthony Neff, Yuri Fuji, Alvin Sewe, Sascha Manteufel
Joint Venture Partner: Bregman + Hamann Architects

Structural Engineer: ARUP (London), Halsall Associates
Mechanical Engineer: ARUP, TMP Consulting Engineers
Electrical Engineer: ARUP, MBII
Landscape Architect: Quinn Design Associates
Acoustic Consultant: Valcoustics
Life Safety Consultant: Leber/Rubes
Rain, Water, and Snow Management Consultant: RWDI
Heritage Consultant: ERA
Contractor: Vanbots Construction
Royal Ontario Museum Chair, 2007
Client: Royal Ontario Museum
Principal: Yama Karim
Design Team: Michael Ashley
Manufacturer: Nienkämper

The L Tower and Sony Centre for the Performing Arts
Toronto, Canada, 2011
Client: Castlepoint Realty Partners, Fernbrook Homes,
Cityzen Development Group
Principal: Carla Swickerath
Design Team: Jason Jimenez, Raul Correa-Smith, Wan-Chi
Chang, Ilana Altman, Jens Jessen
Association with Architect of Record: Page + Steele Architects
Structural Engineer: Jablonsky, Ast and Partners
Mechanical/Electrical/Plumbing Engineer: Smith and Andersen
Consulting Engineering
Landscape Architect: Claude Cormier Architectes Paysagistes
Heritage Consultant: ERA

Hermitage-Guggenheim Vilnius Museum
Vilnius, Lithuania, 2008
Client: Hermitage-Guggenheim Museum
Principal: Yama Karim
Competition Team: Michael Ashley, Kristian Fosholt, Jared
Olmsted, Sascha Manteufel, Alvin Sewe, Matthew Young
Structural Engineer: ARUP (New York)
Mechanical/Electrical/Plumbing Engineer: ARUP

Zlota 44
Warsaw, Poland, 2010
Client: Orco Property Group
Principal: Yama Karim
Design Team: Joe Rom, Brian Melcher, Maxi Spina, Wendy
James, Jennifer Milliron, Toralf Sümmchen, Scharlotte Hopf
Association with Architect of Record: Artchitecture SP ZOO
Project Management: Reese Architekten
Structural Engineer: ARUP (New York/Warsaw)
Mechanical/Electrical/Plumbing Engineer: ARUP